Copyright © 1993 Kidsbooks, Inc.
7004 N. California Ave.
Chicago, IL 60645

All rights reserved including the right
of reproduction in whole or in part in any form.

Manufactured in the United States of America

THE GIANT STATUES OF EASTER ISLAND

On Easter Sunday, 1722, Dutch Admiral Jacob Roggeveen sailed to a small island in the South Pacific. When he went ashore he discovered more than 600 giant statues, some over 40 feet tall, carved from stone. In 1947, Thor Heyerdahl, a Norwegian archeologist, led an expedition to discover how the statues got there.

See if you can find all the things you did or didn't know about the Giant Statues of Easter Island in this picture. Don't forget to look for the following fun things, too.

- ☐ Artist
- ☐ Banana leaves
- ☐ Bone
- ☐ Broom
- ☐ Carrot
- ☐ Drum
- ☐ Duck
- ☐ Flower
- ☐ Flying bat
- ☐ Football
- ☐ Graduate
- ☐ Guitar
- ☐ Key
- ☐ Ladder
- ☐ Mouse
- ☐ Owl
- ☐ Paintbrush
- ☐ Painted eggs (3)
- ☐ Party hats (2)
- ☐ Pelican
- ☐ Periscope
- ☐ Photographer
- ☐ Ring
- ☐ Rocking chair
- ☐ Skateboard
- ☐ Stars (3)
- ☐ Telescope
- ☐ Toucan
- ☐ Truck
- ☐ Unicorn
- ☐ Wagon
- ☐ Water bucket
- ☐ Witch

What was used to carve the statues?
What was the name of Heyerdahl's raft?

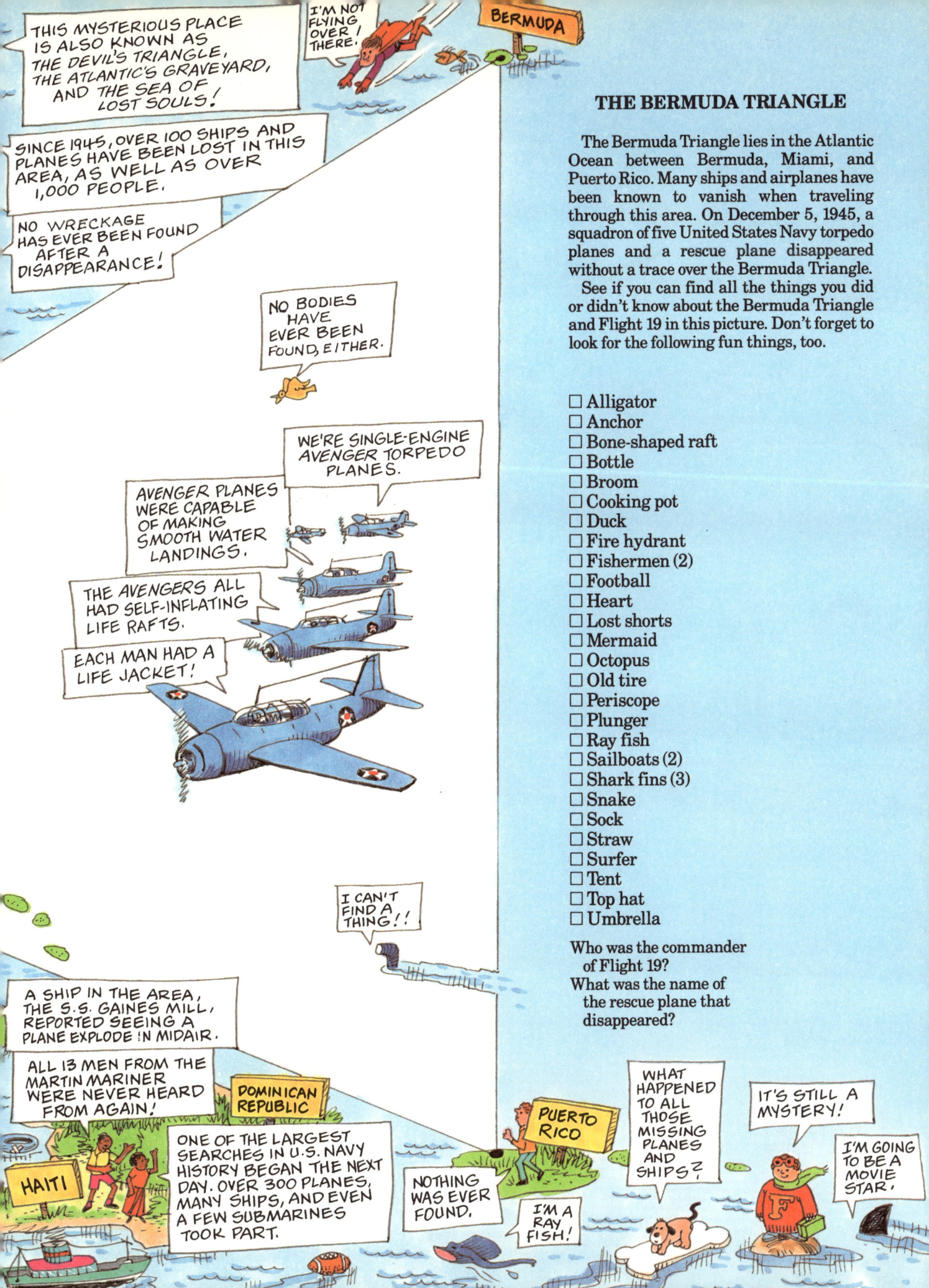

LOCH NESS MONSTER

In 1933, a Scottish couple was driving along the new modern road on the northern shore of the Loch Ness lake. Suddenly, their attention was drawn to the center of the lake. They claimed they saw an enormous animal "rolling and plunging" in the water. Since that day there have been over 3,000 reported sightings of the Loch Ness monster.

See if you can find all the things you did or didn't know about the Loch Ness monster in this picture. Don't forget to look for the following fun things, too.

- ☐ Astronaut
- ☐ Balloons (4)
- ☐ Bone
- ☐ Bucket
- ☐ Cameras (2)
- ☐ Clown
- ☐ Duck
- ☐ Fishbowl
- ☐ Flower
- ☐ Ghost
- ☐ Giraffe
- ☐ Golfer
- ☐ Graduate
- ☐ Lost boot
- ☐ Mailbox
- ☐ Mouse
- ☐ Mummy
- ☐ Net
- ☐ Note-in-a-bottle
- ☐ Periscope
- ☐ Pig
- ☐ Sailboat
- ☐ Santa
- ☐ Shorts
- ☐ Skateboard
- ☐ Star
- ☐ Sword
- ☐ Telescope
- ☐ Top hat
- ☐ Turtle

What is the monster's nickname?
How deep is Loch Ness?

STONEHENGE

Stonehenge is an ancient monument built on Salisbury Plain in Wiltshire, England. For centuries, scientists have puzzled over the circular arrangement of this group of huge, rough-cut stones and holes in the ground. Archeologists believe Stonehenge was shaped and positioned by a group of people over 3,300 years ago without the aid of modern tools and equipment. No one knows exactly how this was accomplished.

See if you can find all the things you did or didn't know about Stonehenge in this picture. Don't forget to look for the following fun things, too.

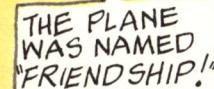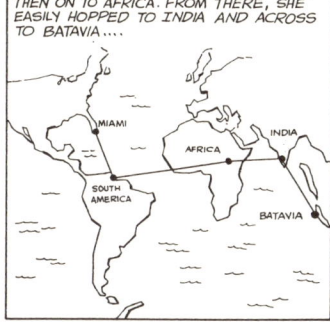

ATLANTIS

The idea of a perfect world—one filled with beauty, peace, and happiness—had kept man searching for the lost island of Atlantis for centuries. Was Atlantis a real place, or just an ancient Egyptian myth made popular by Plato?

See if you can find all the things you did or didn't know about Atlantis in this picture. Don't forget to look for the following fun things, too.

- ☐ Ant
- ☐ Axe
- ☐ Book
- ☐ Chef's hat
- ☐ Chicken
- ☐ Deep-sea diver
- ☐ Deer
- ☐ Elephant
- ☐ Flamingo
- ☐ Frog
- ☐ Guitar
- ☐ Heart
- ☐ Ice-cream cone
- ☐ Kite
- ☐ Lion
- ☐ Mermaid
- ☐ Owl
- ☐ Ox
- ☐ Paintbrush
- ☐ Pelican
- ☐ Periscope
- ☐ Pig
- ☐ Rhinoceros
- ☐ Snail
- ☐ Snake
- ☐ Sock
- ☐ Toucan
- ☐ Turtle
- ☐ Umbrella
- ☐ Unicorn
- ☐ Zebra

Who was Plato?
Some scientists believe Atlantis was what island?

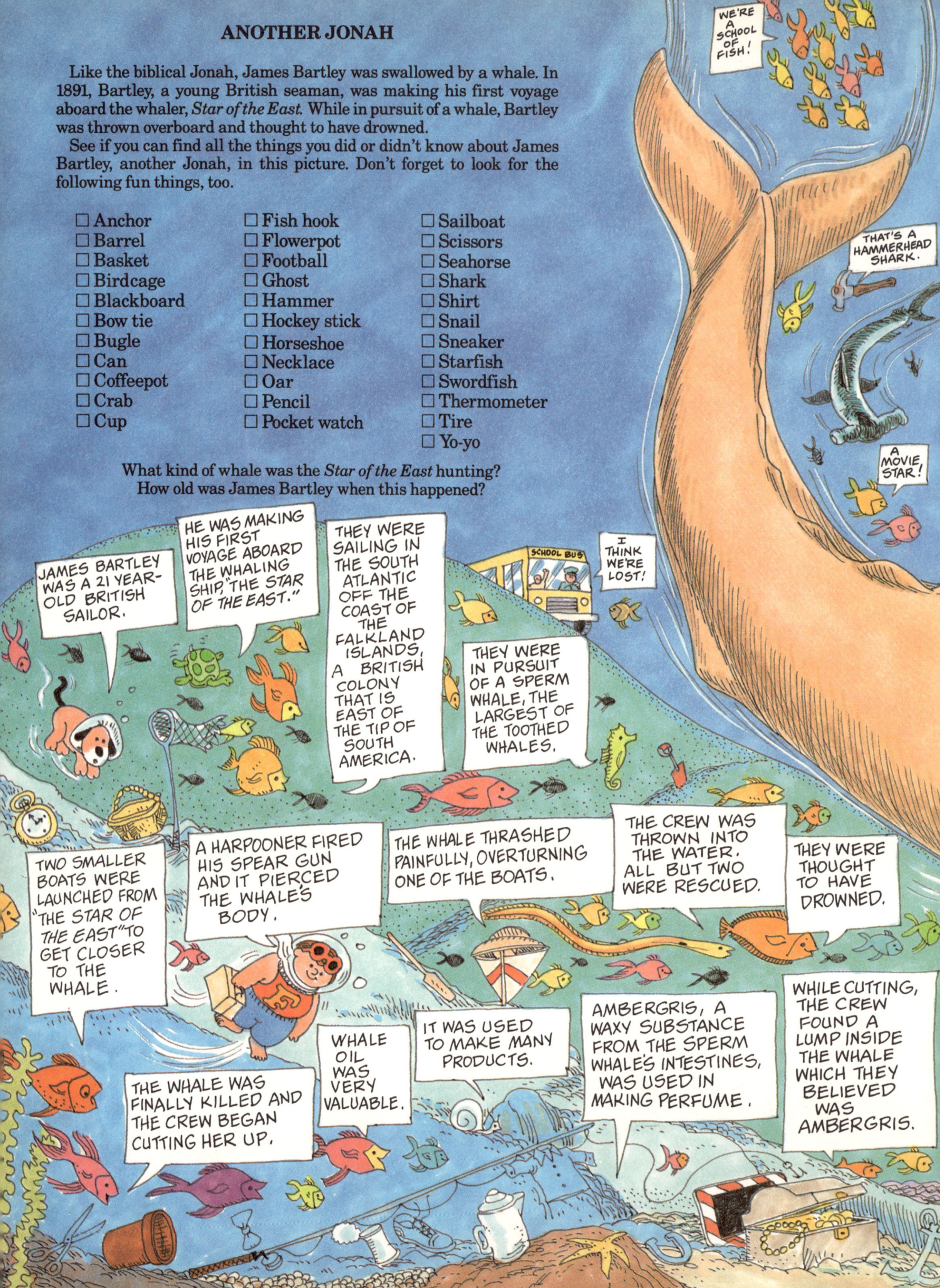

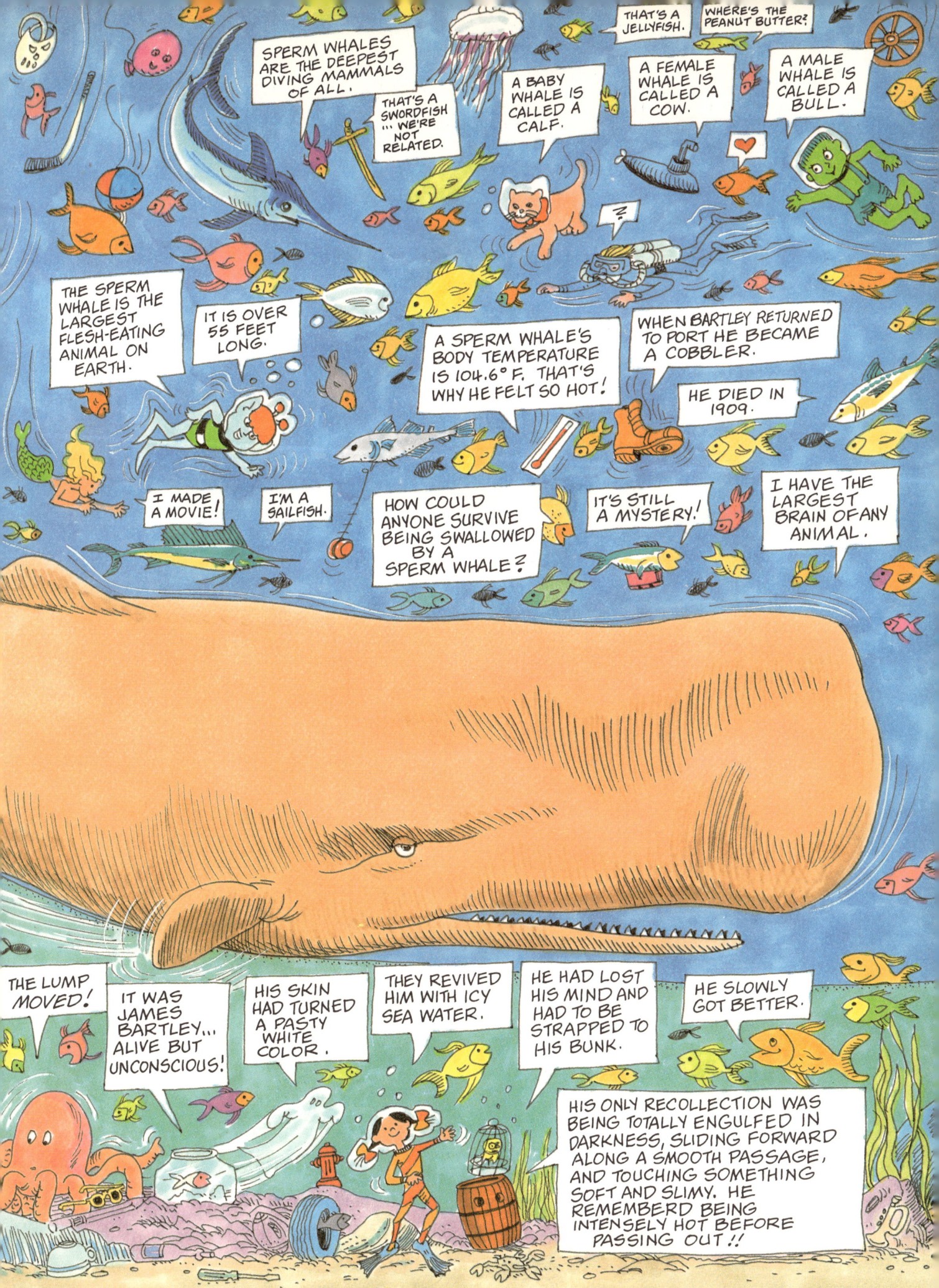

THE TUNGUSKA EXPLOSION

On June 30, 1908, the sky over the icy wilderness of Siberia flashed with a bright streak of light. Suddenly, the earth shook and smoke and fire shot up into the sky reaching a height of 10 miles. This tremendous explosion was recorded around the world.

See if you can find all the things you did or didn't know about the Tunguska Explosion in this picture. Don't forget to look for the following fun things, too.

- ☐ Arrow
- ☐ Bat
- ☐ Bear
- ☐ Bell
- ☐ Birdbath
- ☐ Boot
- ☐ Camel
- ☐ Crayon
- ☐ Crown
- ☐ Cupcake
- ☐ Doll
- ☐ Drum
- ☐ Elephant
- ☐ Envelope
- ☐ Fish
- ☐ Flashlight
- ☐ Football
- ☐ Fork
- ☐ Ghost
- ☐ Heart
- ☐ Hot-air balloon
- ☐ Hot dog
- ☐ Igloo
- ☐ Jack-o'-lantern
- ☐ Key
- ☐ Kite
- ☐ Lips
- ☐ Mailbox
- ☐ Mask
- ☐ Moon face
- ☐ Mouse
- ☐ Pillow
- ☐ Ring
- ☐ Sailboat
- ☐ Skis
- ☐ Snake
- ☐ Tent
- ☐ Tin can
- ☐ Tire
- ☐ Toothbrush
- ☐ Top hat
- ☐ Tree
- ☐ Tulip
- ☐ Turtle
- ☐ TV set
- ☐ Umbrella

When were atomic bombs first produced?
What is a meteorite?

Speech bubbles in illustration:

- On June 30, 1908, the famous Tunguska meteorite crashed into the earth in Siberia.
- Siberia is in Asia. It is a vast, icy wilderness.
- People 466 miles away saw this meteor in full daylight.
- A meteor is a bright streak of light.
- Meteors are known as shooting stars or falling stars because they look like stars falling from the sky.
- Meteorites are chunks of metal or stone that reach the surface of the earth before burning up.
- Friction with the air creates the bright streak of light.
- People felt the earth shake 50 miles away!
- It was estimated to weigh a few hundred tons.
- The fire it caused scorched a 20 mile area of earth.
- Smoke and fire shot up into the sky to a height of 10 miles.
- All over the world, seismographs felt and recorded the explosion.

I Didn't Know That! About How Things Work

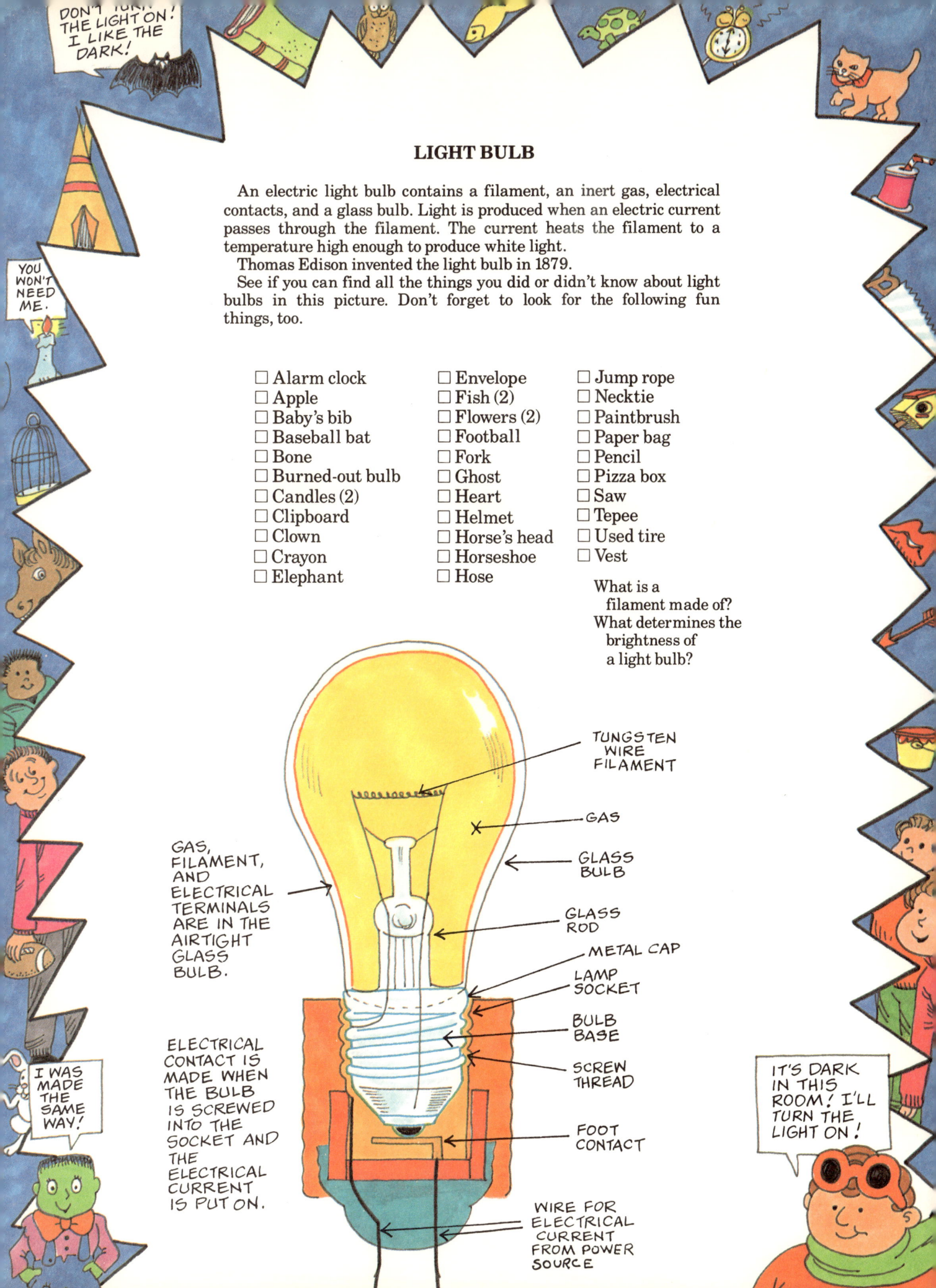

MAKING PAPER

About 5,000 years ago, the Egyptians used a writing material made from a plant called papyrus. Today, from soft tissues to tough cardboard, paper is made chiefly from fibers produced by trees, in large factories called paper mills.

See if you can find all the things you did or didn't know about making paper in this picture. Don't forget to look for the following fun things, too.

- ☐ Balloon
- ☐ Basket
- ☐ Bear
- ☐ Bird
- ☐ Bow and arrow
- ☐ Broom
- ☐ Bucket
- ☐ Cane
- ☐ Carrot
- ☐ Fish
- ☐ Flower
- ☐ Fork
- ☐ Heart
- ☐ Ice-cream cone
- ☐ Key
- ☐ Kite
- ☐ Mouse
- ☐ Mushroom
- ☐ Oilcan
- ☐ Owl
- ☐ Paper airplane
- ☐ Plumber's helper
- ☐ Ring
- ☐ Shopping bag
- ☐ Skier
- ☐ Snowman
- ☐ Telescope
- ☐ Toothbrush
- ☐ Turtles (2)
- ☐ Wizard
- ☐ Worm

What are calendar stacks?
Who invented the kind of paper that we use today?

HELICOPTER

Helicopters can fly straight up or down, forward or backward, sideways, and even hover in place. Because of their mobility they can fly into places that airplanes cannot.

The first helicopter to achieve flight was built in France in 1907. But it was not completely reliable. In 1939, Igor Sikorsky developed the first successful one and the modern era of helicopters began.

See if you can find all the things you did or didn't know about helicopters in this picture. Don't forget to look for the following fun things, too.

- ☐ Balloon
- ☐ Bee
- ☐ Book
- ☐ Butterfly
- ☐ Cactus
- ☐ Camera
- ☐ Candy cane
- ☐ Canteen
- ☐ Flying bat
- ☐ Frog
- ☐ Heart
- ☐ Jack-o'-lantern
- ☐ Lollipop
- ☐ Medal
- ☐ Mouse
- ☐ Oilcan
- ☐ Owl
- ☐ Pail
- ☐ Paper airplane
- ☐ Penguin
- ☐ Periscope
- ☐ Roller skates
- ☐ Sailboat
- ☐ Schoolbag
- ☐ Screwdriver
- ☐ Squirrel
- ☐ Tennis racket
- ☐ Turtle
- ☐ Worm

How many main rotor blades do most helicopters have?
What gives a helicopter its power?

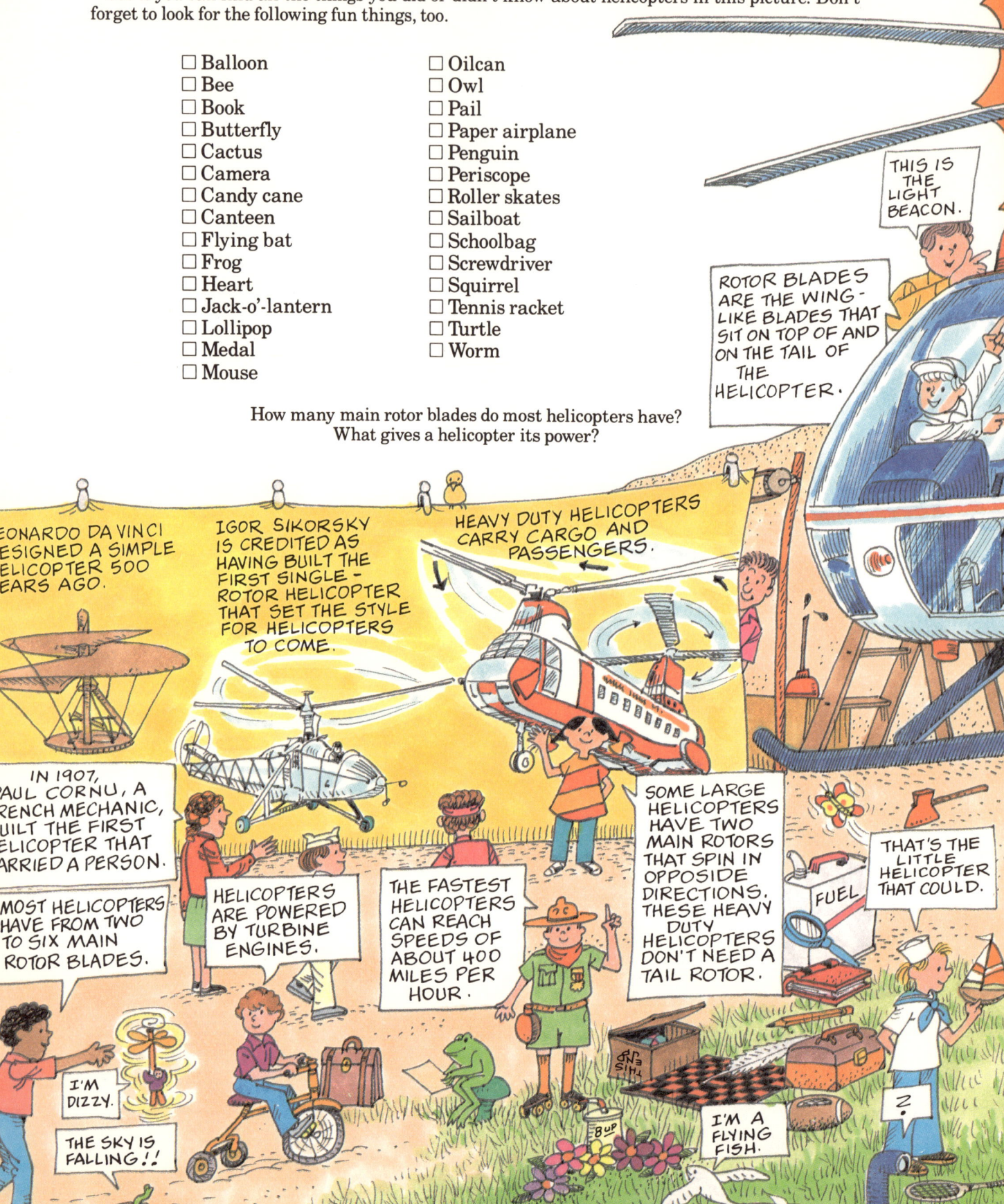

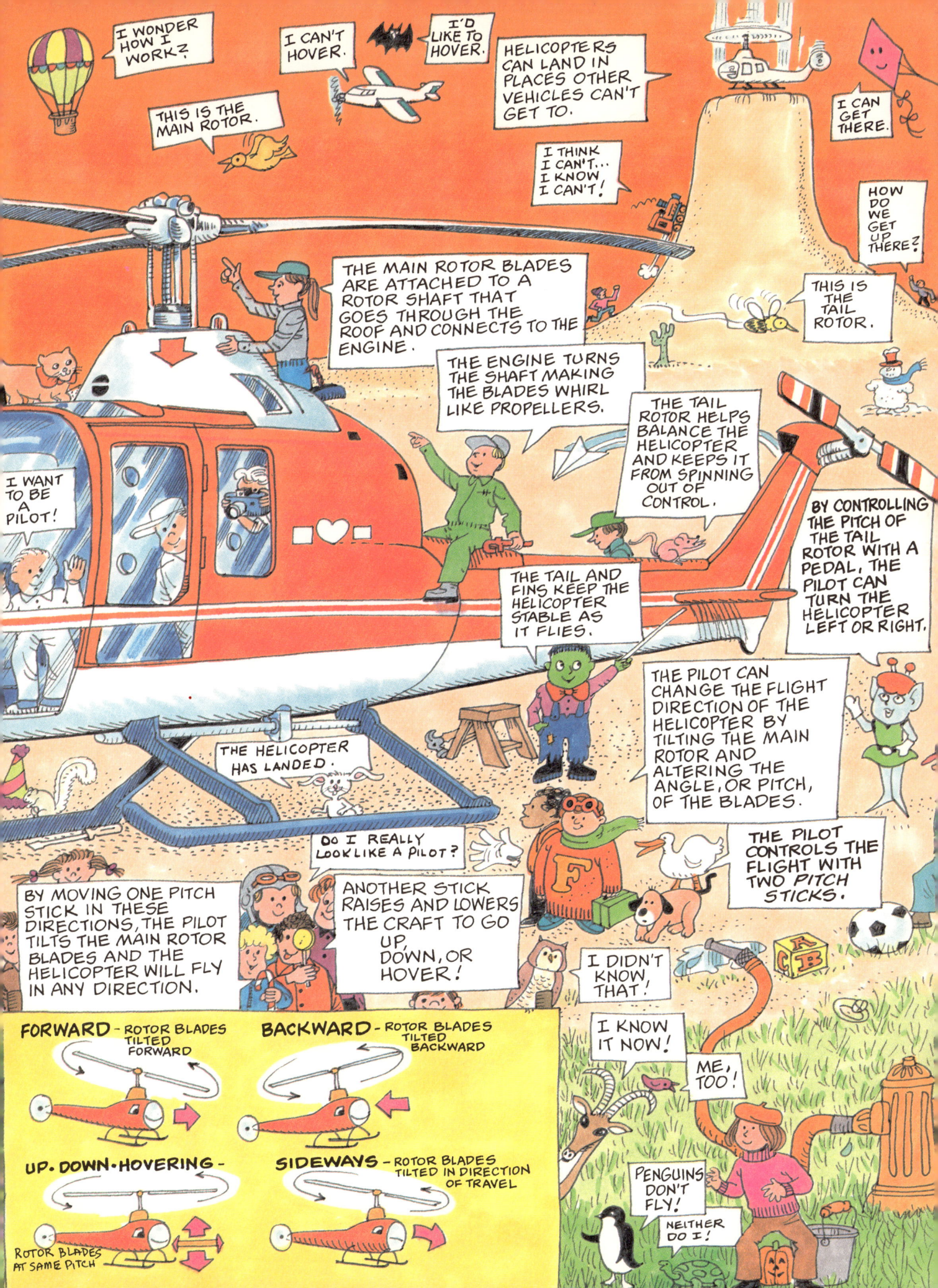

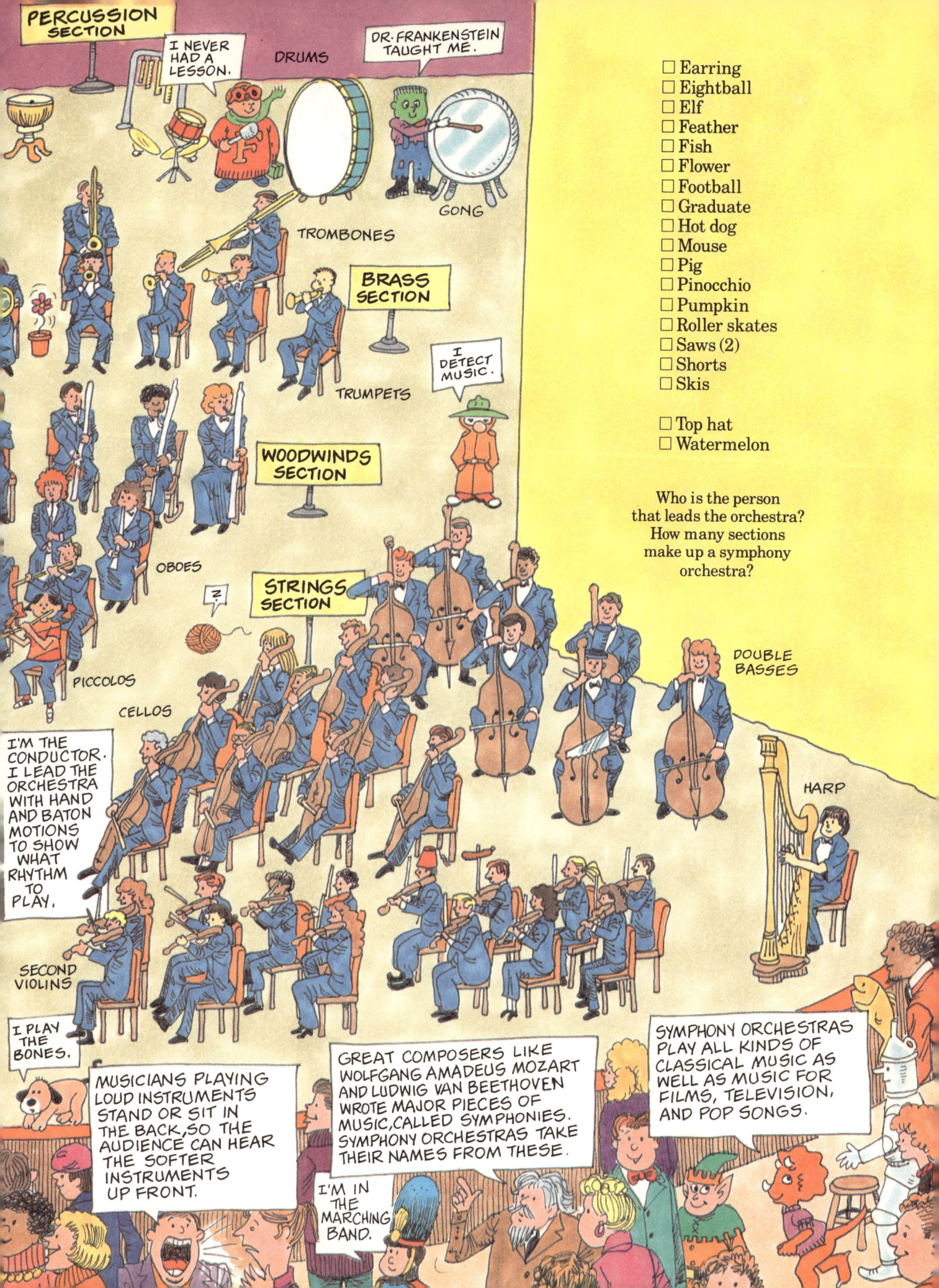

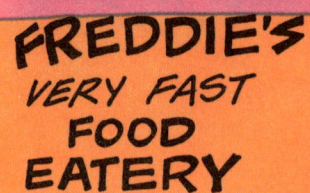

MICROWAVE OVEN

Microwaves are waves of invisible heat energy. Unlike ordinary ovens that use gas or electric heat, a microwave oven uses microwaves to heat, defrost, and cook food.

See if you can find all the things you did or didn't know about microwaves in this picture. Don't forget to look for the following fun things, too.

- ☐ Ball
- ☐ Ballerina
- ☐ Bone
- ☐ Book
- ☐ Bottle
- ☐ Cane
- ☐ Cape
- ☐ Chef's hat
- ☐ Deer
- ☐ Elf
- ☐ Fan
- ☐ Football helmet
- ☐ Fork
- ☐ Hard hat
- ☐ Knife
- ☐ Lion
- ☐ Moose
- ☐ Mouse
- ☐ Napkin holder
- ☐ Necktie
- ☐ Olive
- ☐ Owl
- ☐ Pizza
- ☐ Santa Claus
- ☐ Shark fin
- ☐ Straw
- ☐ Tinman
- ☐ Top hat
- ☐ Turtle
- ☐ Wristwatch

How do microwaves cook food?
Why shouldn't metal containers be used in microwave ovens?

HOW DOES FREDDIE KEEP THINGS SO HOT AND COOK THINGS SO FAST?

HE USES A MICROWAVE OVEN!

MICROWAVE BEAMS ARE PRODUCED WHEN ELECTRICITY PASSES THROUGH A DEVICE CALLED A MAGNETRON.

THE BEAMS STRIKE A SPINNING FAN THAT SENDS THE MICROWAVES IN MANY DIRECTIONS. THESE WAVES PASS THROUGH THE FOOD CONTAINER AND INTO THE FOOD.

SINCE MICROWAVES CANNOT PASS THROUGH METAL, THE WAVES BOUNCE OFF THE LINED METAL OVEN AND PASS BACK AND FORTH THROUGH THE FOOD, OVER AND OVER AGAIN.

I DETECT FAST FOOD!

WHERE'S SANTA?

IN ORDINARY OVENS, THE HEAT DOES NOT PASS THROUGH FOOD, BUT COOKS IT FROM THE OUTSIDE IN. THIS IS WHY A STEAK CAN BE BROWN ON THE OUTSIDE AND RED ON THE INSIDE.

METAL FOOD CONTAINERS SHOULD NOT BE USED IN MICROWAVE OVENS BECAUSE THE WAVES CANNOT PASS THROUGH METAL.

MICROWAVES HEAT THE MOLECULES OF WATER WITHIN THE FOOD, COOKING IT EVENLY AND QUICKLY THROUGHOUT.

THE TURNTABLE SPINS SLOWLY CAUSING THE FOOD TO ROTATE WITHIN THE OVEN. THIS HELPS FOR MORE EVEN COOKING OF THE FOOD.

Ahhh!

A SMALL COMPUTER IN THE MICROWAVE OVEN CAN BE SET TO AUTOMATICALLY COOK FOOD AT THE RIGHT TEMPERATURE FOR THE RIGHT AMOUNT OF TIME.

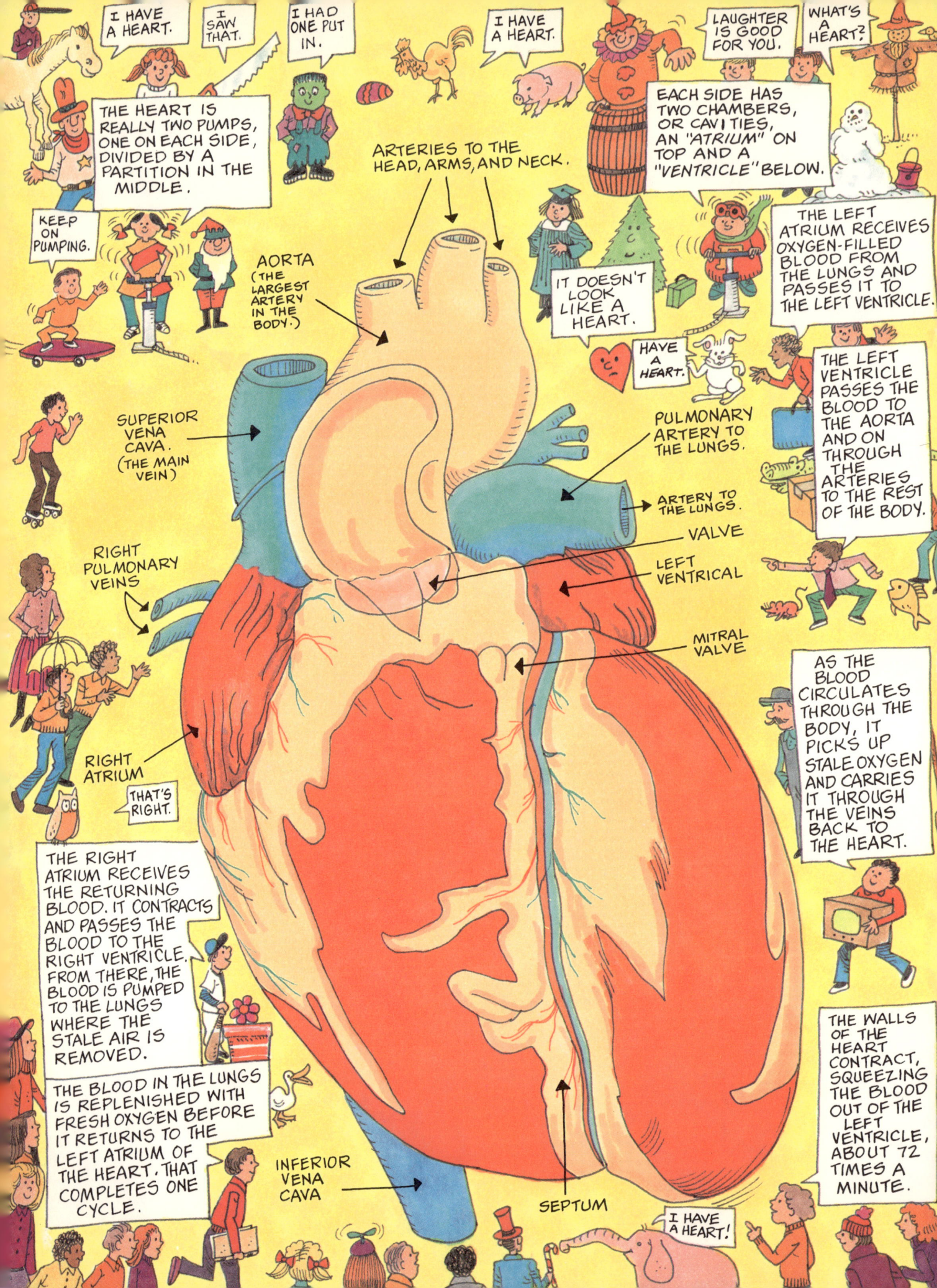

HUMAN HEART

A heart is a muscular pump that circulates blood through the blood vessels. The blood carries nourishment and oxygen to every part of the body. In one year the human heart pumps about 650,000 gallons of blood, enough to fill 50 swimming pools!

See if you can find all the things you did or didn't know about the human heart in this picture. Don't forget to look for the following fun things, too.

- ☐ Ball
- ☐ Banana peel
- ☐ Barrel
- ☐ Baseball bat
- ☐ Book
- ☐ Broom
- ☐ Candy cane
- ☐ Chicken
- ☐ Dracula
- ☐ Drum
- ☐ Duck
- ☐ Fish
- ☐ Flower
- ☐ Joggers (2)
- ☐ Lion
- ☐ Microscope
- ☐ Mouse
- ☐ Moustache
- ☐ Owl
- ☐ Pillow
- ☐ Propeller
- ☐ Roller skates
- ☐ Saw
- ☐ Singer
- ☐ Skateboard
- ☐ Stars (2)
- ☐ Top hat
- ☐ TV set
- ☐ Umbrella
- ☐ Worm

What are the heart's chambers called?
Approximately how long does it take for the blood to travel throughout the body?

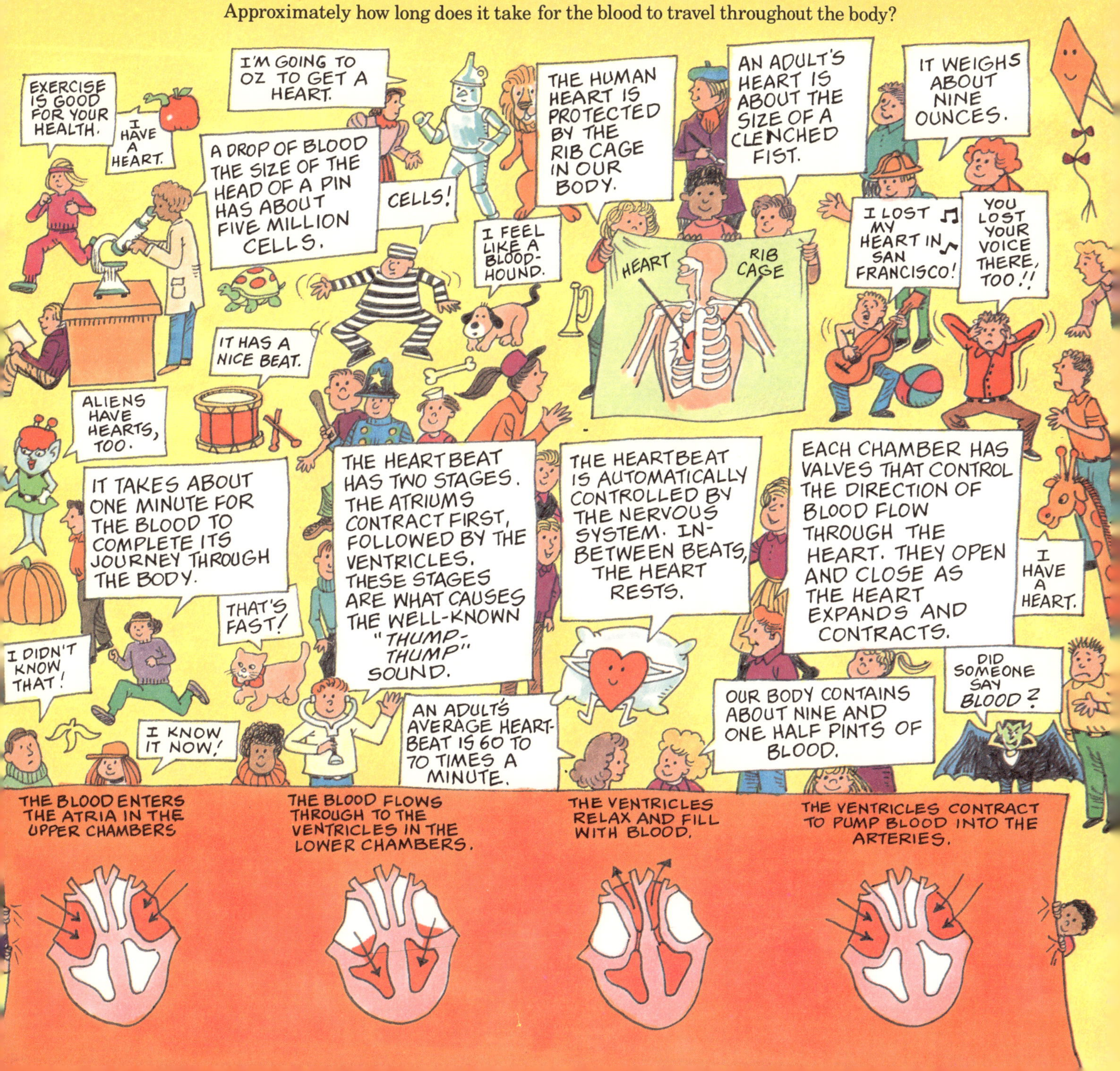

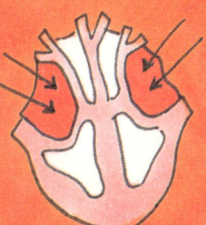
THE BLOOD ENTERS THE ATRIA IN THE UPPER CHAMBERS

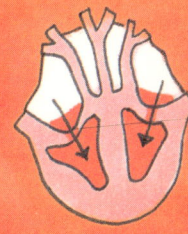
THE BLOOD FLOWS THROUGH TO THE VENTRICLES IN THE LOWER CHAMBERS.

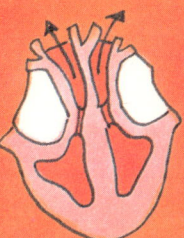
THE VENTRICLES RELAX AND FILL WITH BLOOD.

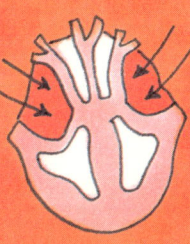
THE VENTRICLES CONTRACT TO PUMP BLOOD INTO THE ARTERIES.

SOLAR ENERGY

Solar energy is power produced by the sun. It can be used to heat and purify water, give power to engines, and produce electricity. Five hundred and fifty billion tons of coal would have to be burned in order to equal the amount of solar energy received by the earth in only one day!

See if you can find all the things you did or didn't know about solar power in this picture. Don't forget to look for the following fun things, too.

- ☐ Apple
- ☐ Arrow
- ☐ Baseball
- ☐ Basketball hoop
- ☐ Bone
- ☐ Brush
- ☐ Buckets (2)
- ☐ Doghouse
- ☐ Duck
- ☐ Earmuffs
- ☐ Fire hydrant
- ☐ Flower
- ☐ Football
- ☐ Ghost
- ☐ Hammer
- ☐ Heart
- ☐ Helmet
- ☐ Kite
- ☐ Mailbox
- ☐ Newspaper
- ☐ Rabbit
- ☐ Screwdriver
- ☐ Star
- ☐ Tepee
- ☐ Turtle
- ☐ Umbrella
- ☐ Umpire
- ☐ Watering can
- ☐ Worm

What is solar power most commonly used for?
Why are the insides of solar panels painted black?

AIRPLANE

Airplanes are fascinating pieces of machinery that soar through the air. Whether passenger, private, or military, they all operate under the same aerodynamic principles.

The first power-driven flight was made by the Wright brothers at Kitty Hawk, North Carolina in 1903.

See if you can find all the things you did or didn't know about airplanes in this picture. Don't forget to look for the following fun things, too.

- ☐ "X-1"
- ☐ Acrobat
- ☐ Banana
- ☐ Bowling ball
- ☐ Broom
- ☐ Elephant
- ☐ Fishing pole
- ☐ Flowers (3)
- ☐ Flying carpet
- ☐ Flying horse
- ☐ Flying saucer
- ☐ Football
- ☐ Ghost
- ☐ Glider
- ☐ Hamburger
- ☐ Hang glider
- ☐ Kite
- ☐ Mouse
- ☐ Paper airplane
- ☐ Pencil
- ☐ Pinwheel
- ☐ Pizza
- ☐ Sailboat
- ☐ Seaplane
- ☐ Sled
- ☐ Stars (2)
- ☐ Superheroes (2)
- ☐ Surfboard
- ☐ Turtle
- ☐ Umbrella
- ☐ Yo-yo

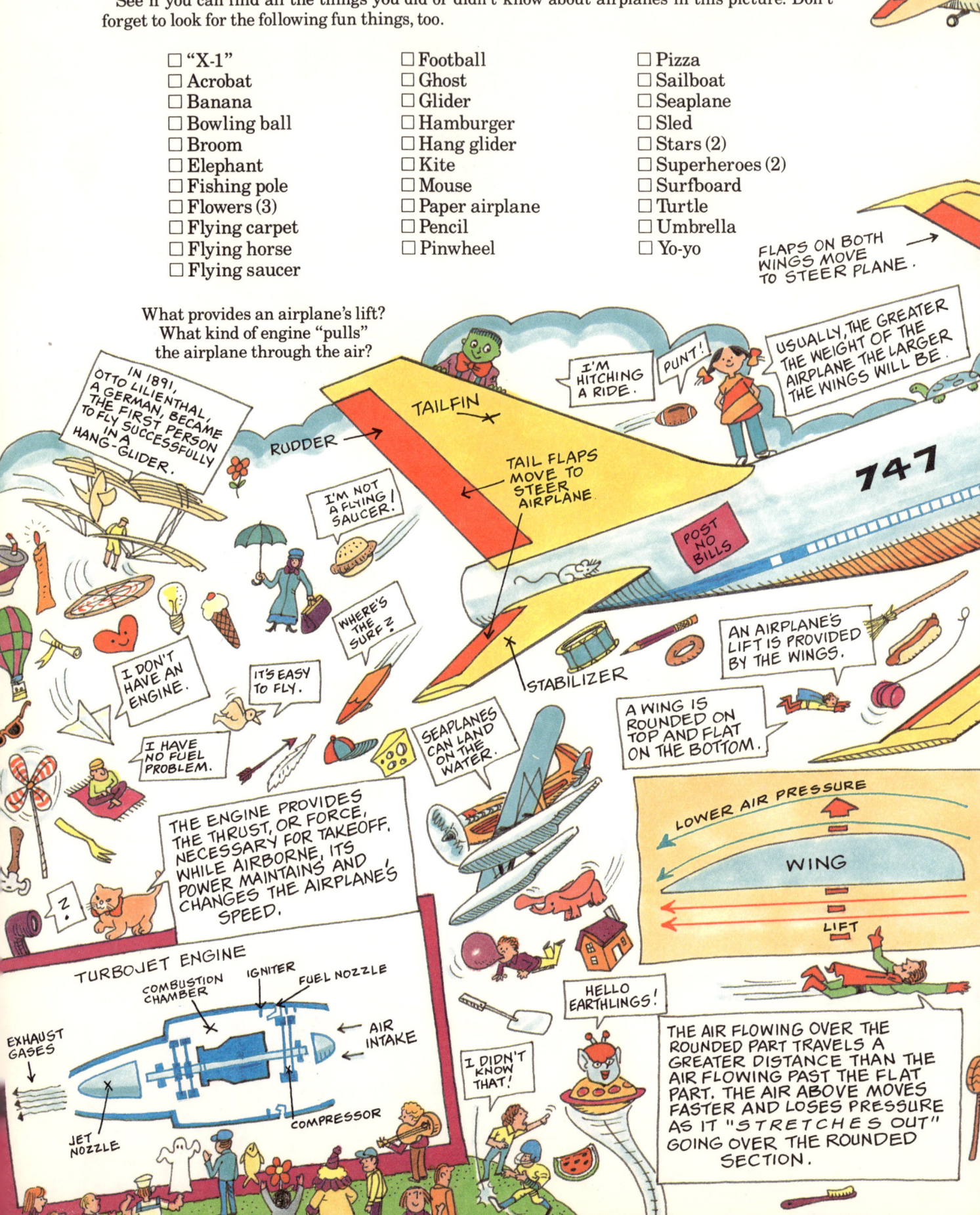

LASERS

A laser is a device that intensifies or increases light. It produces a thin beam of light, stronger than sunlight, that can burn a hole through diamond or steel.

The first operational laser was built in 1960.

See if you can find all the things you did or didn't know about lasers in this picture. Don't forget to look for the following fun things, too.

- ☐ Apple
- ☐ Book
- ☐ Cheerleader
- ☐ Chicken
- ☐ Clock
- ☐ Drum
- ☐ Electrodes (2)
- ☐ Envelope
- ☐ Fish tank
- ☐ Flamingo
- ☐ Football
- ☐ Frog
- ☐ Globe
- ☐ Hot dog
- ☐ Little Red Riding Hood
- ☐ Mouse
- ☐ Necktie
- ☐ Orangutan
- ☐ Painted egg
- ☐ Paper airplane
- ☐ Parrot
- ☐ Roller skates
- ☐ Stapler
- ☐ Stethoscope
- ☐ Straw
- ☐ Thermometer
- ☐ Umbrella
- ☐ Vase

Name two types of lasers.
What are some of the uses of laser beams?

SWIMMING

On a hot summer day, is there anything more refreshing than swimming in a pool, lake, pond, ocean, or river? Swimming is one of the most popular forms of recreation, a wonderful exercise for keeping fit, and an exciting international sport.

See if you can find all the things you did or didn't know about swimming in this picture. Don't forget to look for the following fun things, too.

- ☐ Backpack
- ☐ Birdbath
- ☐ Book
- ☐ Cactus
- ☐ Divers (2)
- ☐ Fisherman
- ☐ Flamingo
- ☐ Flying bat
- ☐ Football helmet
- ☐ Heart
- ☐ Lost sock
- ☐ Mark Spitz
- ☐ Mermaids (2)
- ☐ Monkey
- ☐ Oilcan
- ☐ Owl
- ☐ Pencil
- ☐ Robot
- ☐ Roller skater
- ☐ Rubber ducky
- ☐ Sailboat
- ☐ Sandcastle
- ☐ Shark fin
- ☐ Skunk
- ☐ Submarine
- ☐ Superhero
- ☐ Surfer
- ☐ Tarzan

Name the American swimmer who won nine gold medals in the 1968 and 1972 Olympics?
Who was the first woman to swim the English Channel?

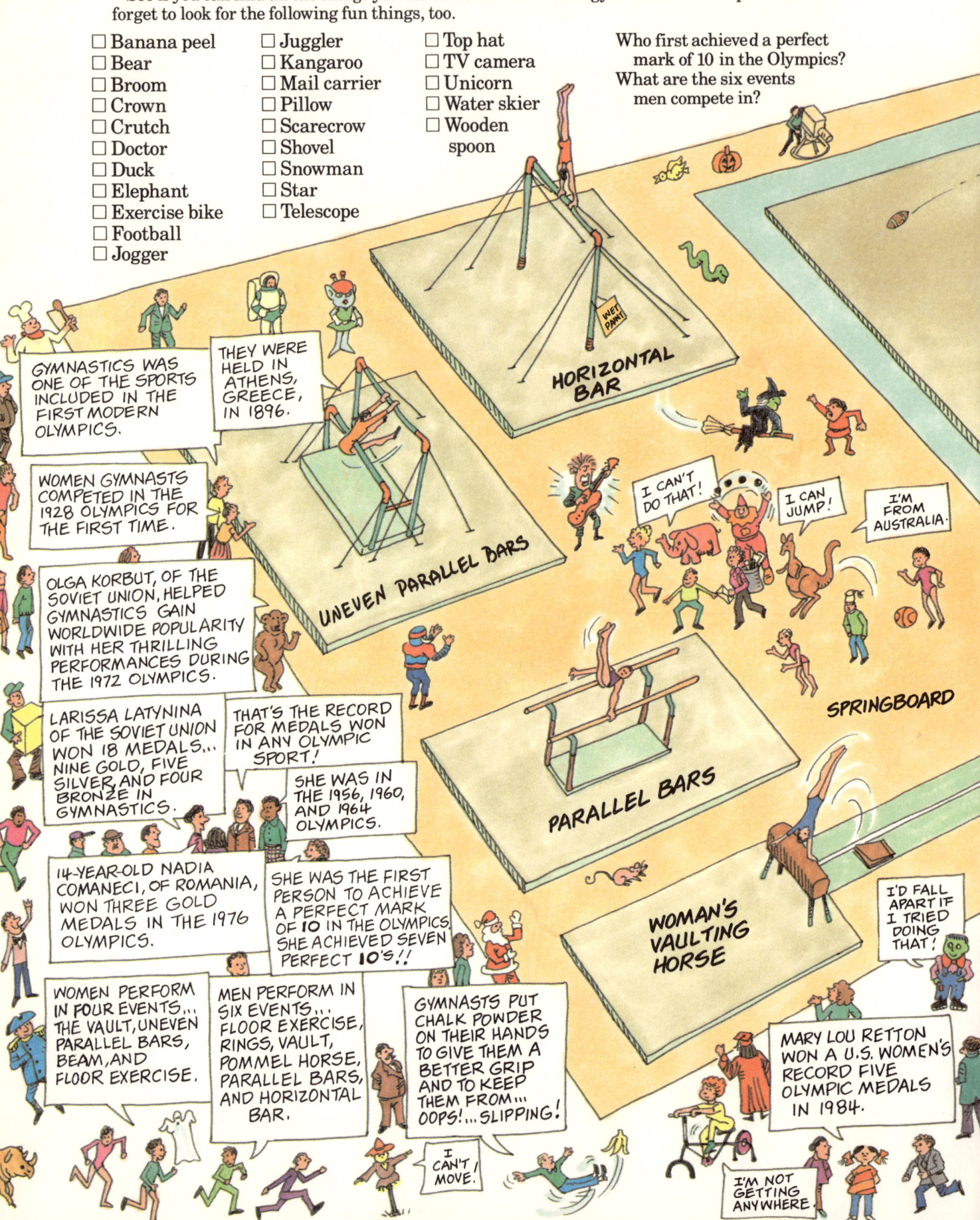

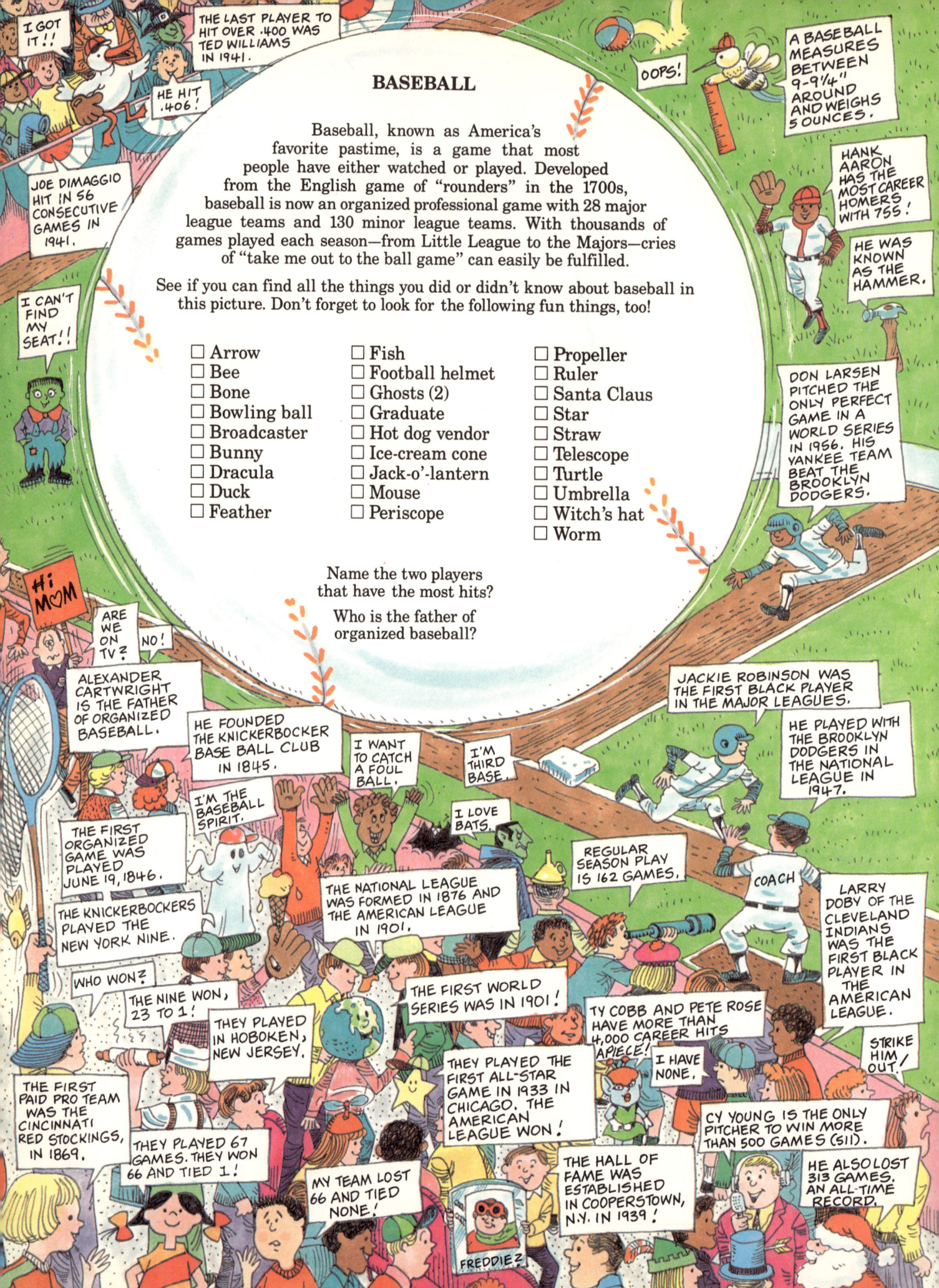

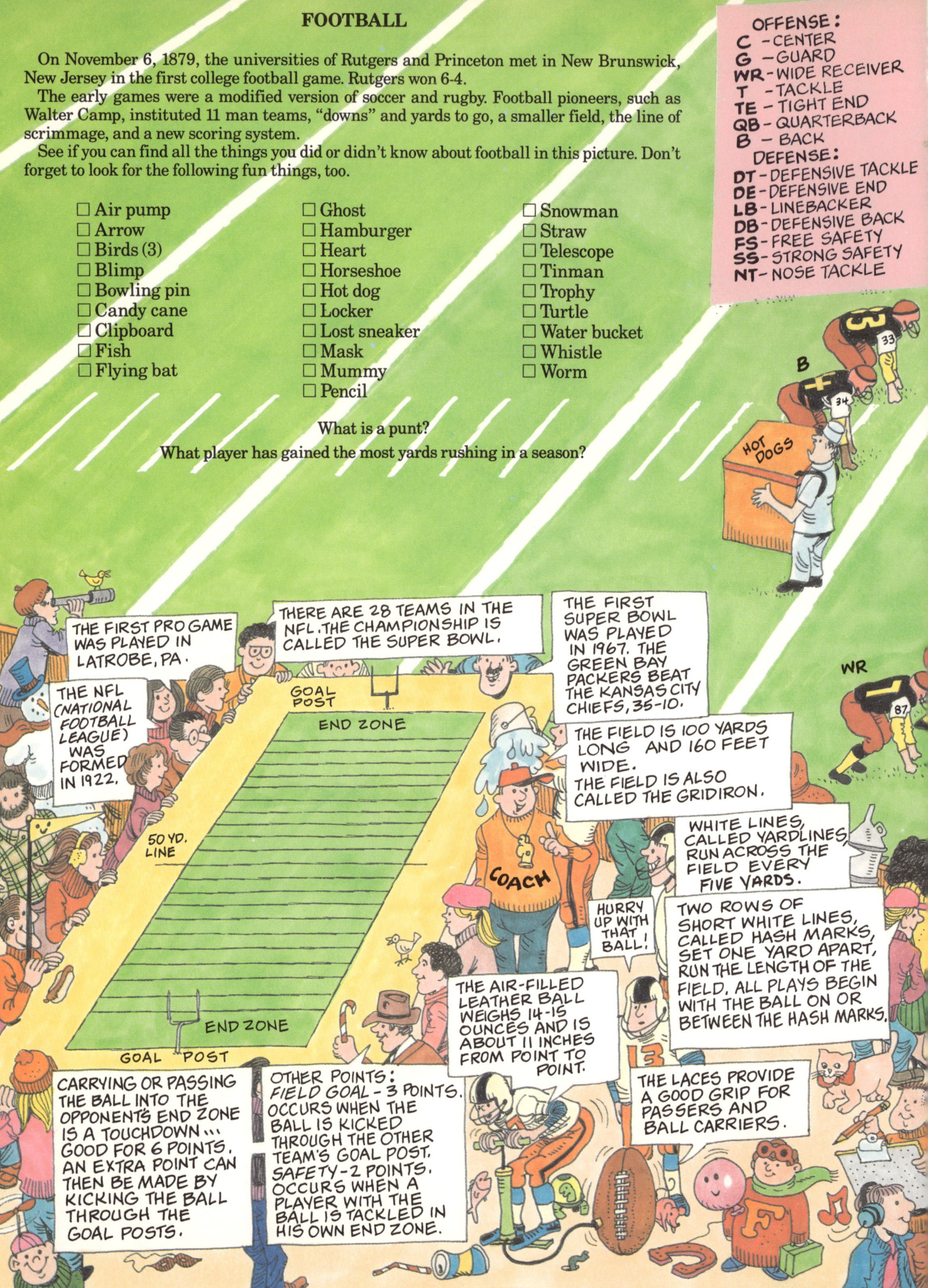

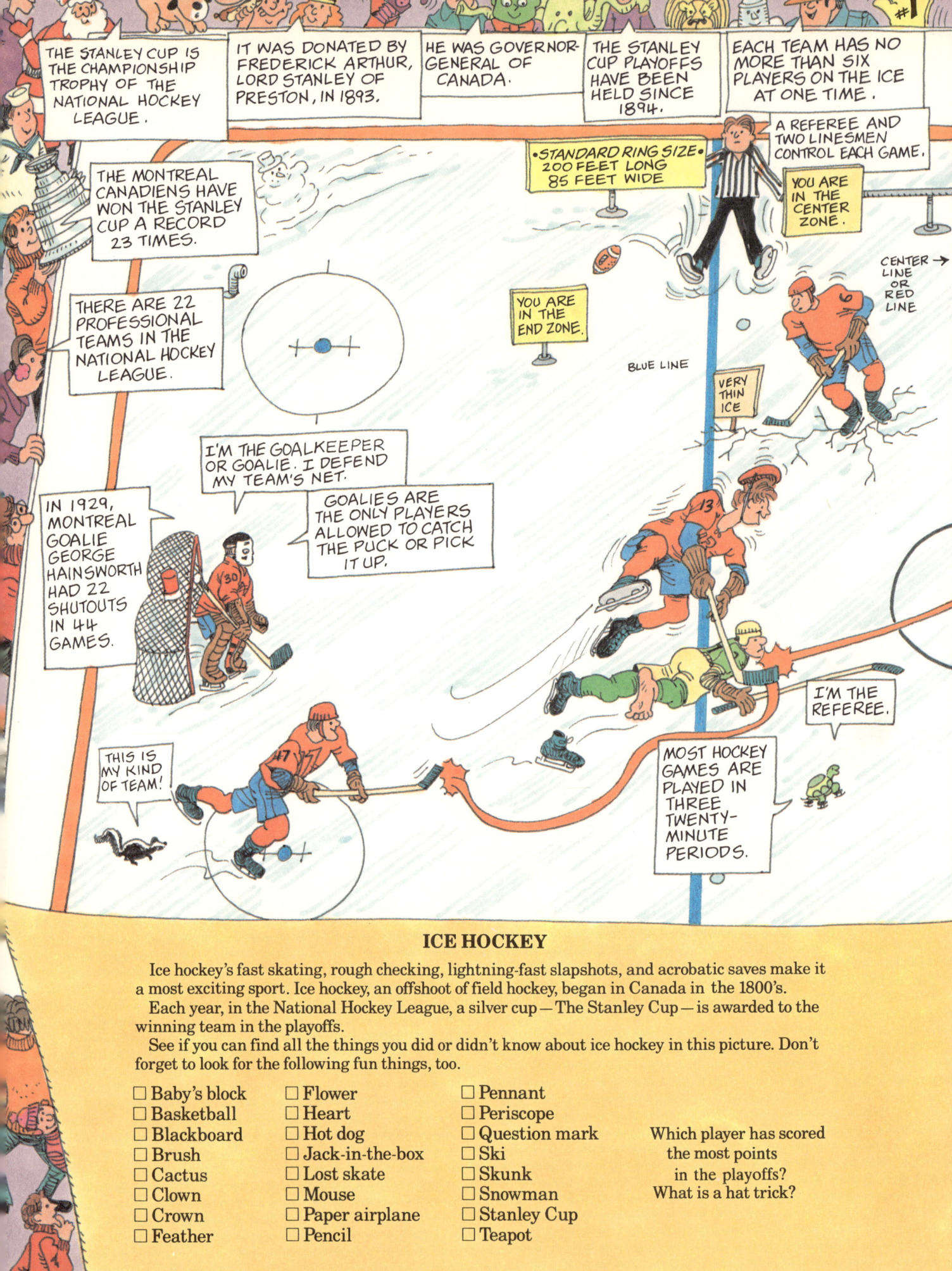

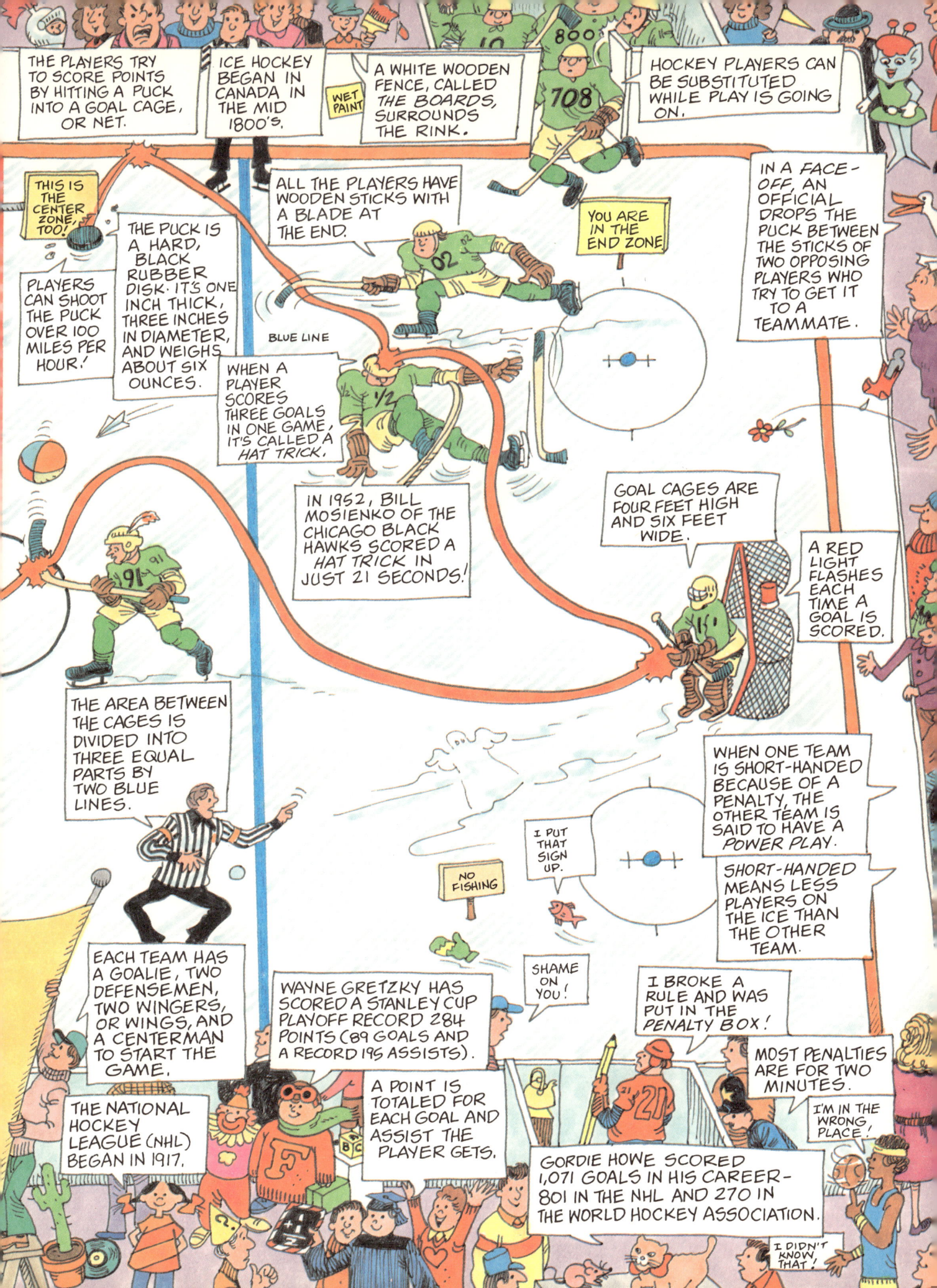

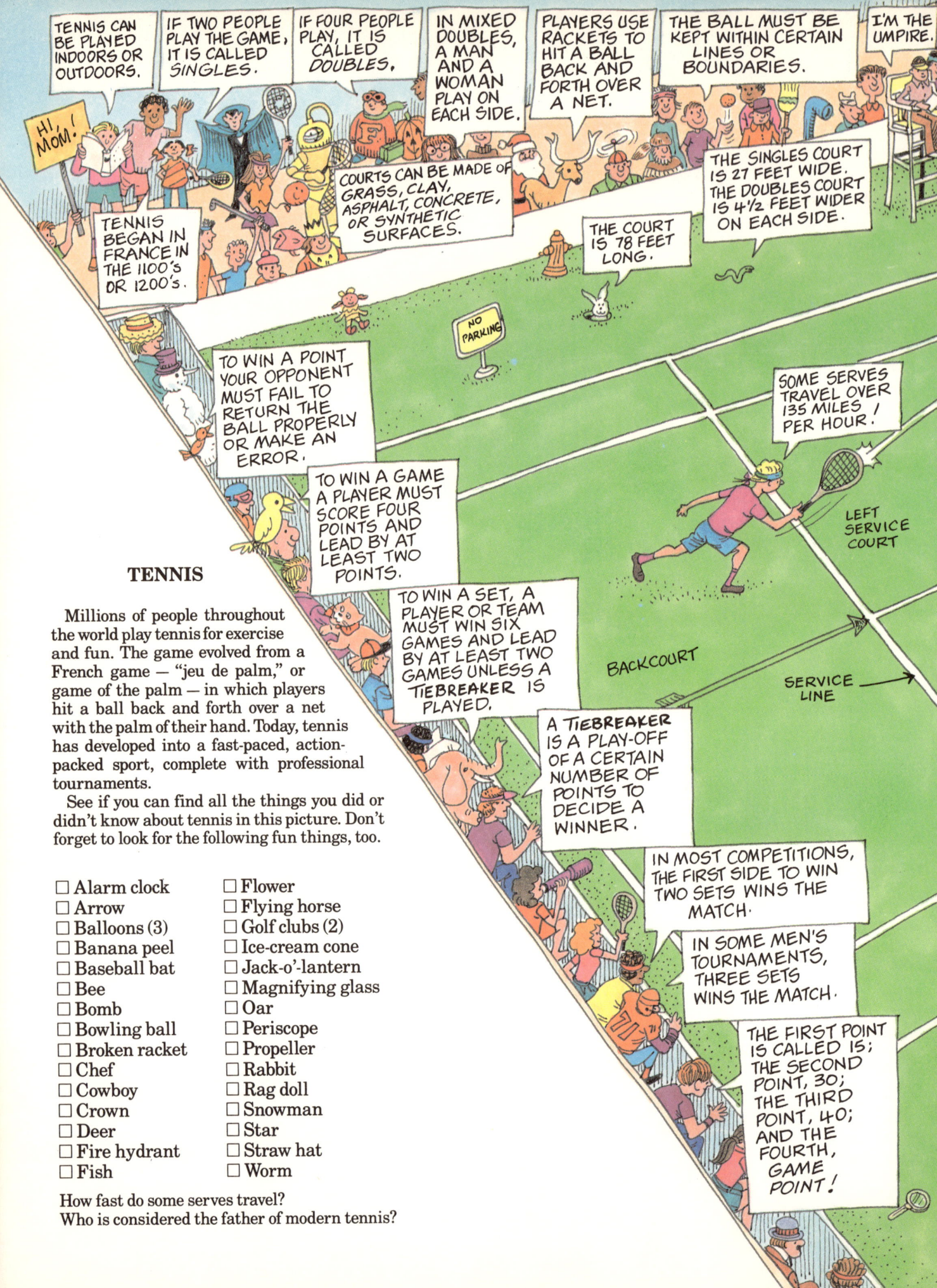

TRACK AND FIELD

Track and field is a sport in which men and women compete in athletic events featuring running, throwing, and jumping. Track events consist of a series of races over various distances ranging from 60 meters to a marathon. Field events measure an athlete's ability to throw and jump.

See if you can find all the things you did or didn't know about track and field in this picture. Don't forget to look for the following fun things, too.

- ☐ Ball of yarn
- ☐ Balloon
- ☐ Birdcage
- ☐ Bomb
- ☐ Candle
- ☐ Chef's hat
- ☐ Count Dracula
- ☐ Deliveryman
- ☐ Duck
- ☐ Elephant
- ☐ Fish
- ☐ Flying bat
- ☐ Football player
- ☐ Helicopter
- ☐ Ice-cream cone
- ☐ Mummy
- ☐ Ostrich
- ☐ Painted egg
- ☐ Periscope
- ☐ Pig
- ☐ Rabbit
- ☐ Roller skater
- ☐ Snake
- ☐ Surfboard
- ☐ Thief
- ☐ Tinman
- ☐ Tuba
- ☐ Turtle
- ☐ Umbrella
- ☐ Weightlifter

How long is a marathon? Name the four throwing events.

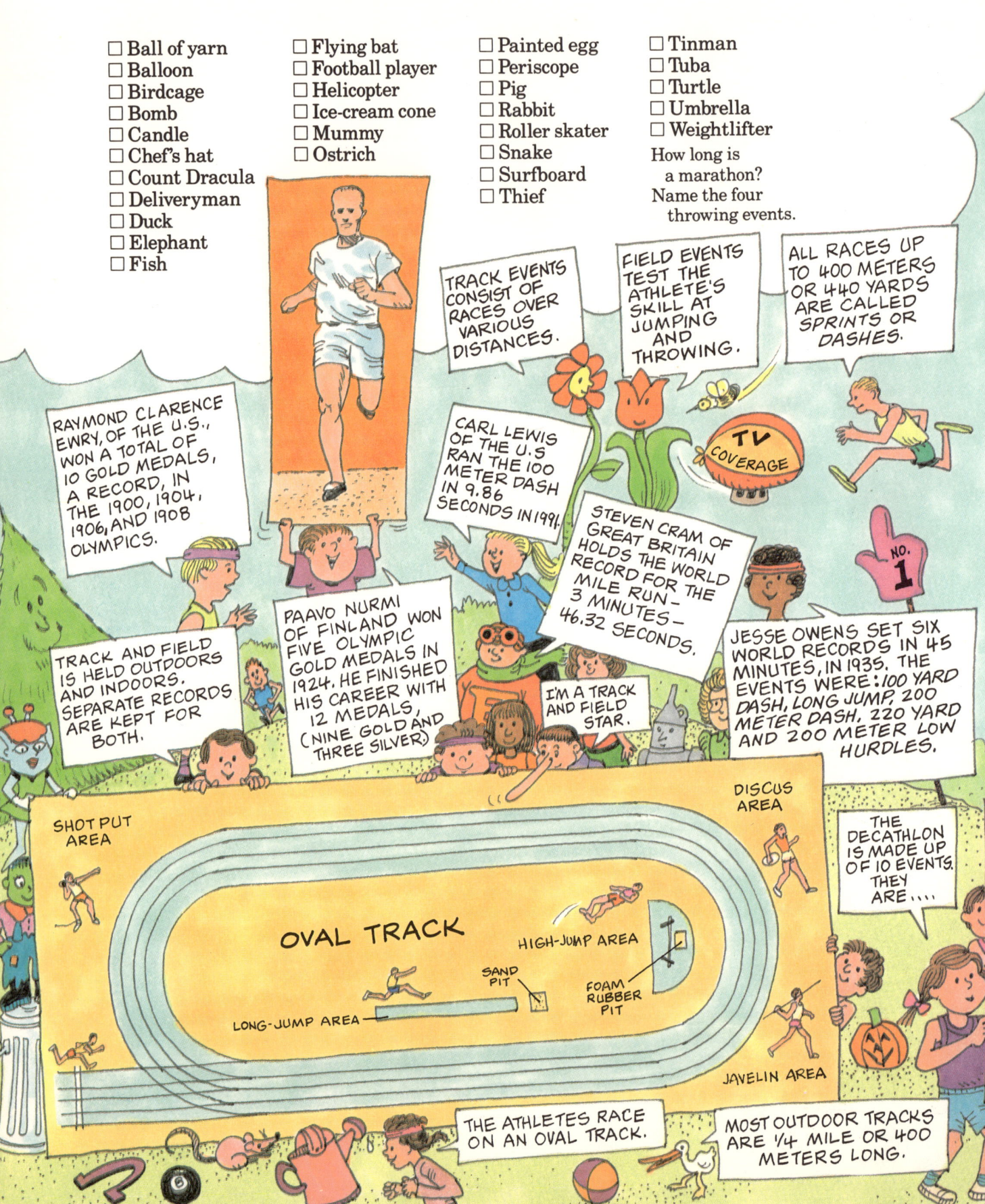

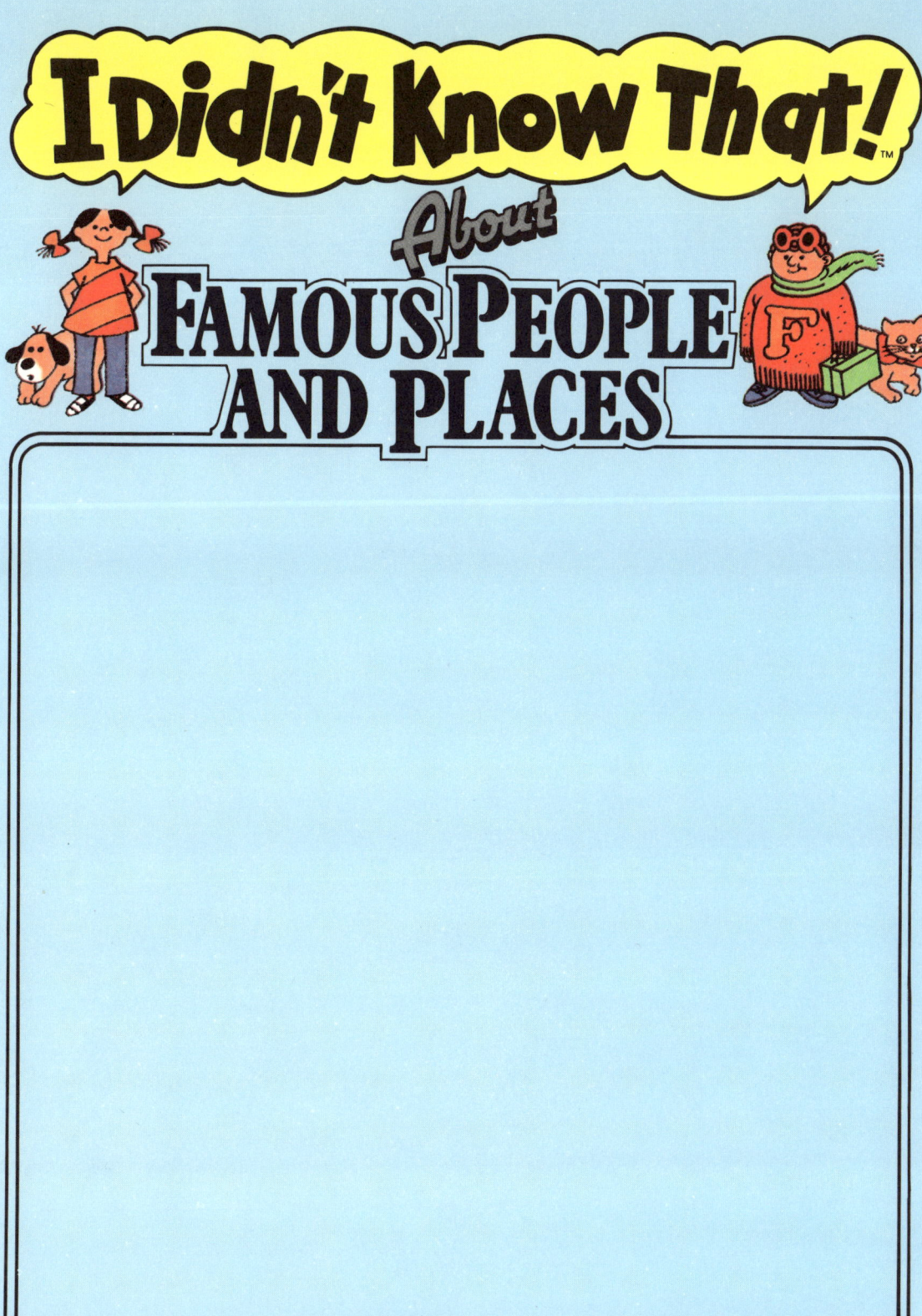

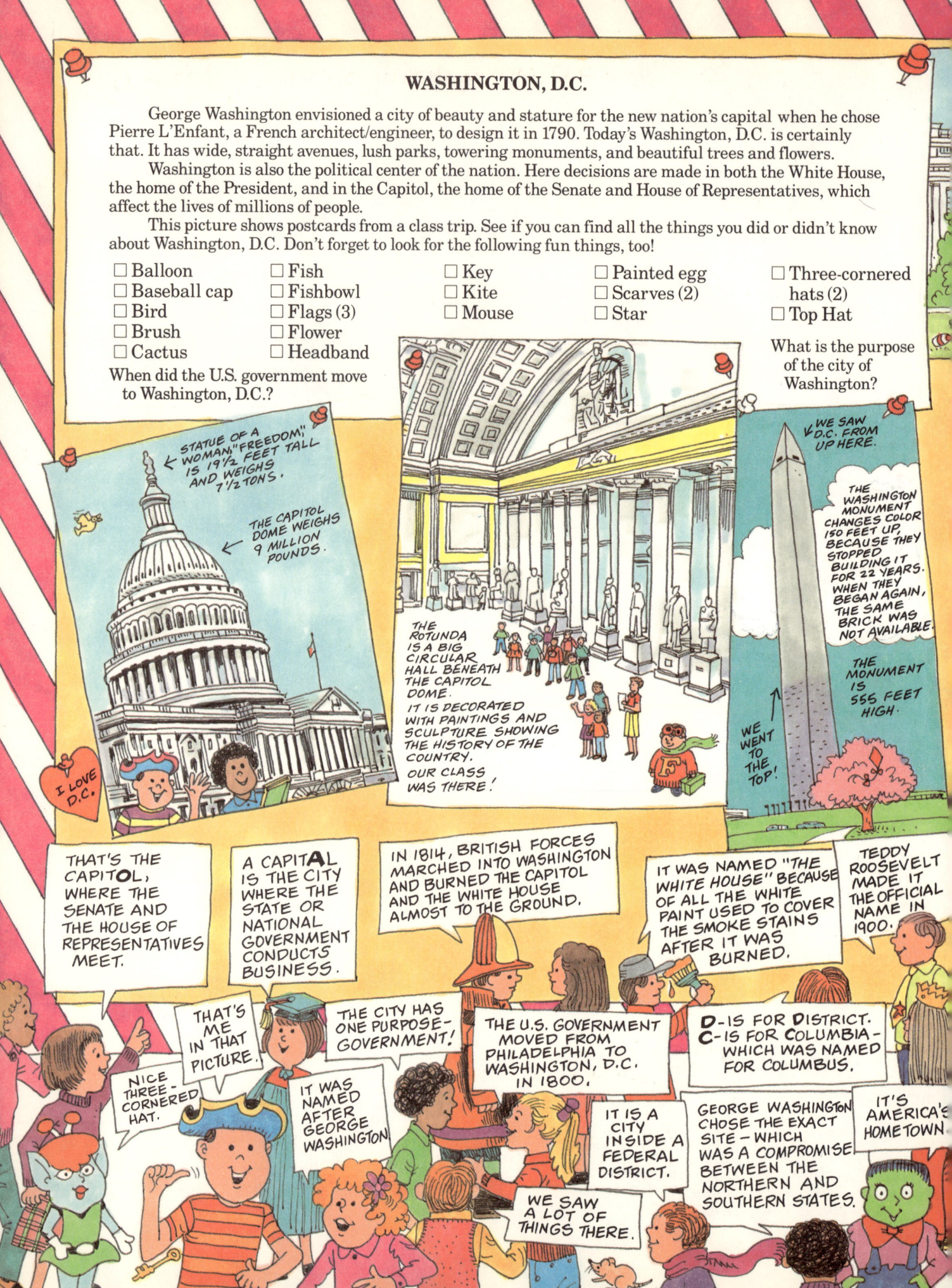

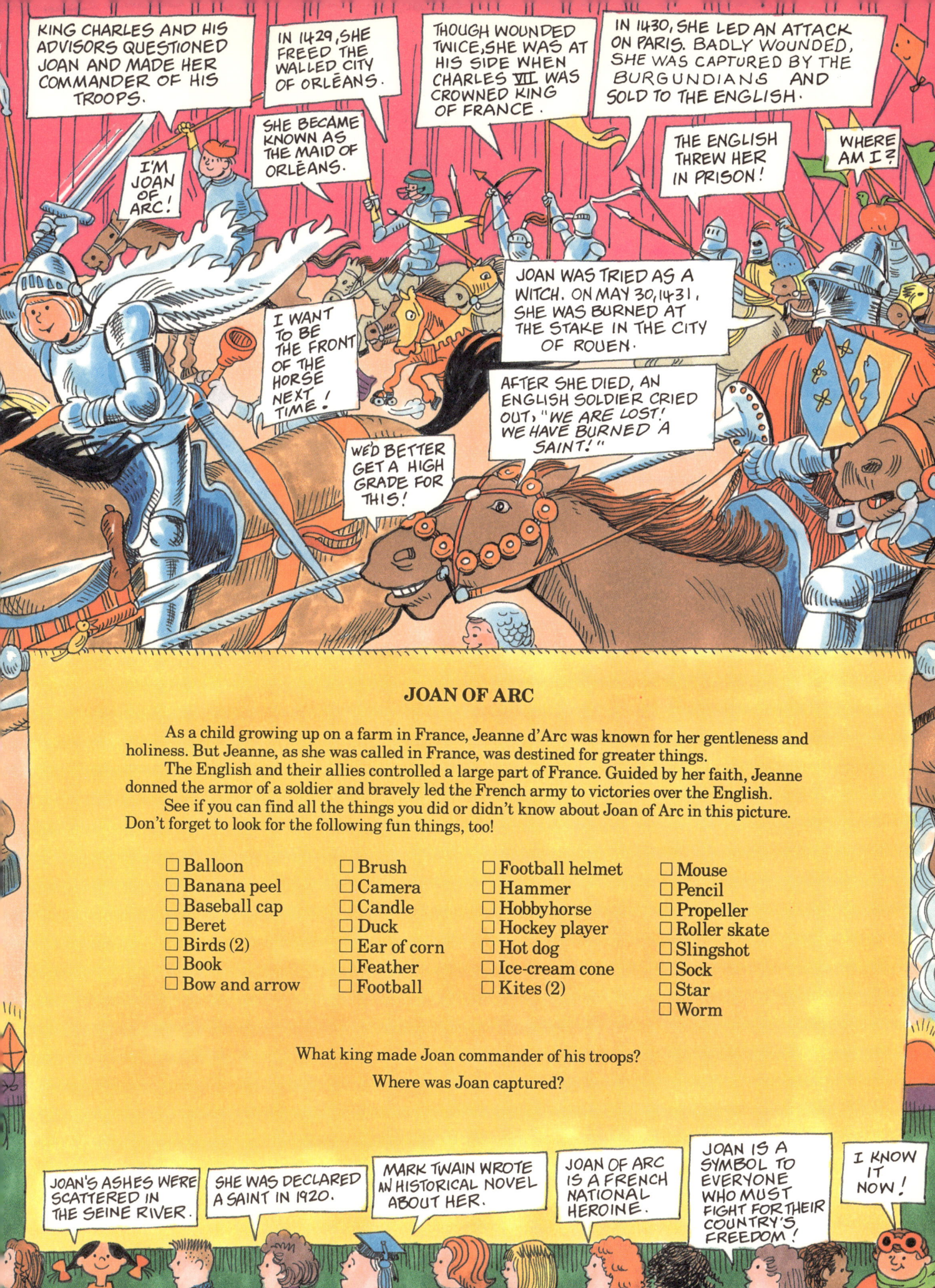

NEW YORK CITY

New York City is the largest city in the United States and the fifth largest in the world. It is a universal center for art, fashion, architecture, finance, publishing, and more. A great deal of what happens in New York affects what happens around the country and even around the world!

See if you can find all the things you did or didn't know about New York City in this picture. Don't forget to look for the following fun things, too!

- ☐ Airplanes (2)
- ☐ Apple
- ☐ Baseball
- ☐ Bird
- ☐ Blimp
- ☐ Book
- ☐ Boom box
- ☐ Container ship
- ☐ Diver
- ☐ Ferry
- ☐ Fish
- ☐ Flower
- ☐ Flying saucer
- ☐ Football
- ☐ Ghost
- ☐ Heart
- ☐ Helicopter
- ☐ Hot-air balloon
- ☐ King Kongs (2)
- ☐ Kite
- ☐ Parachutist
- ☐ Periscope
- ☐ Rocking chair
- ☐ Rowboat
- ☐ Star
- ☐ Telescope
- ☐ Tire
- ☐ Top hat
- ☐ Tugboat
- ☐ Worm

Who first settled New York?
When was New York City the nation's capital?

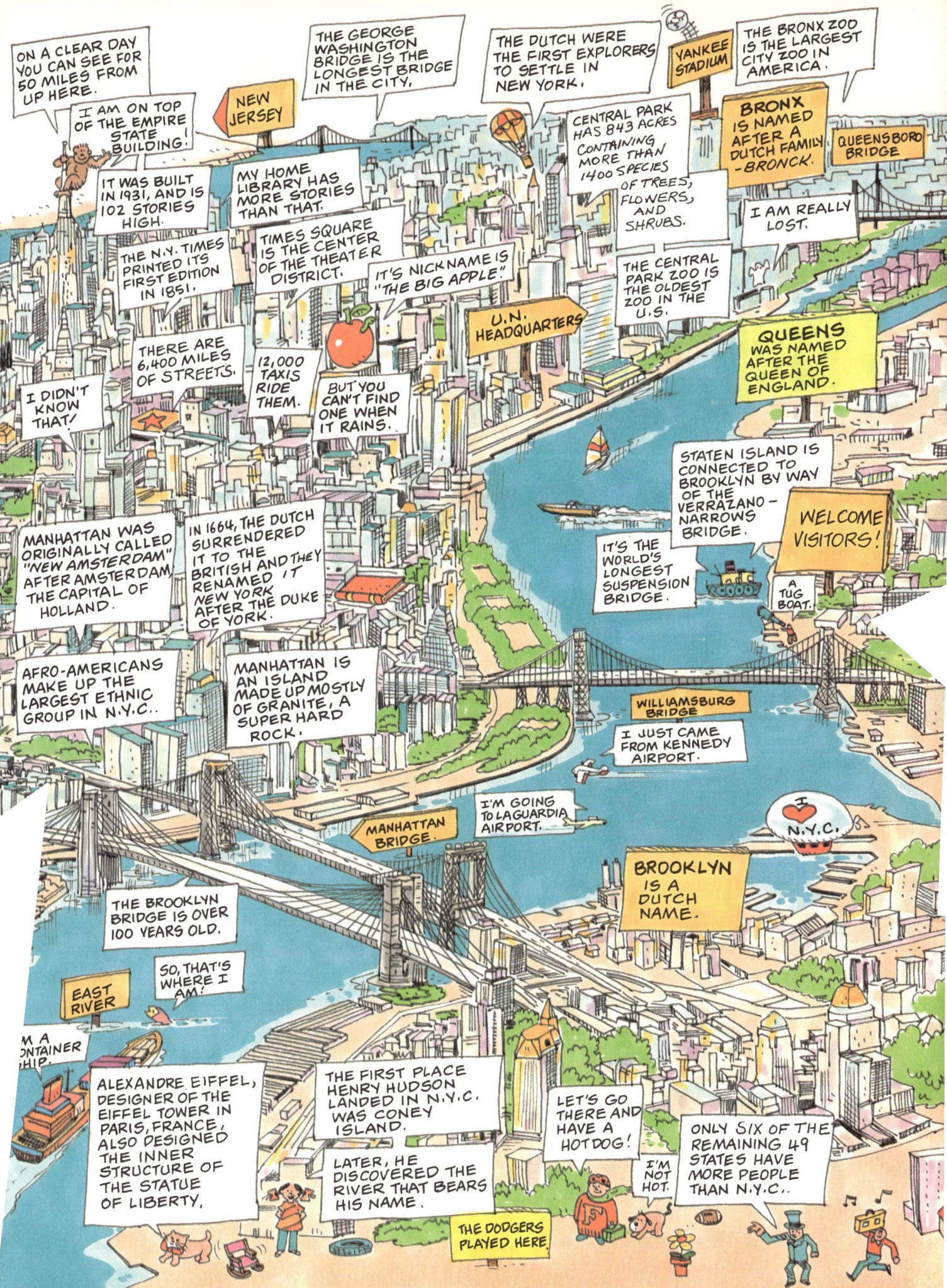

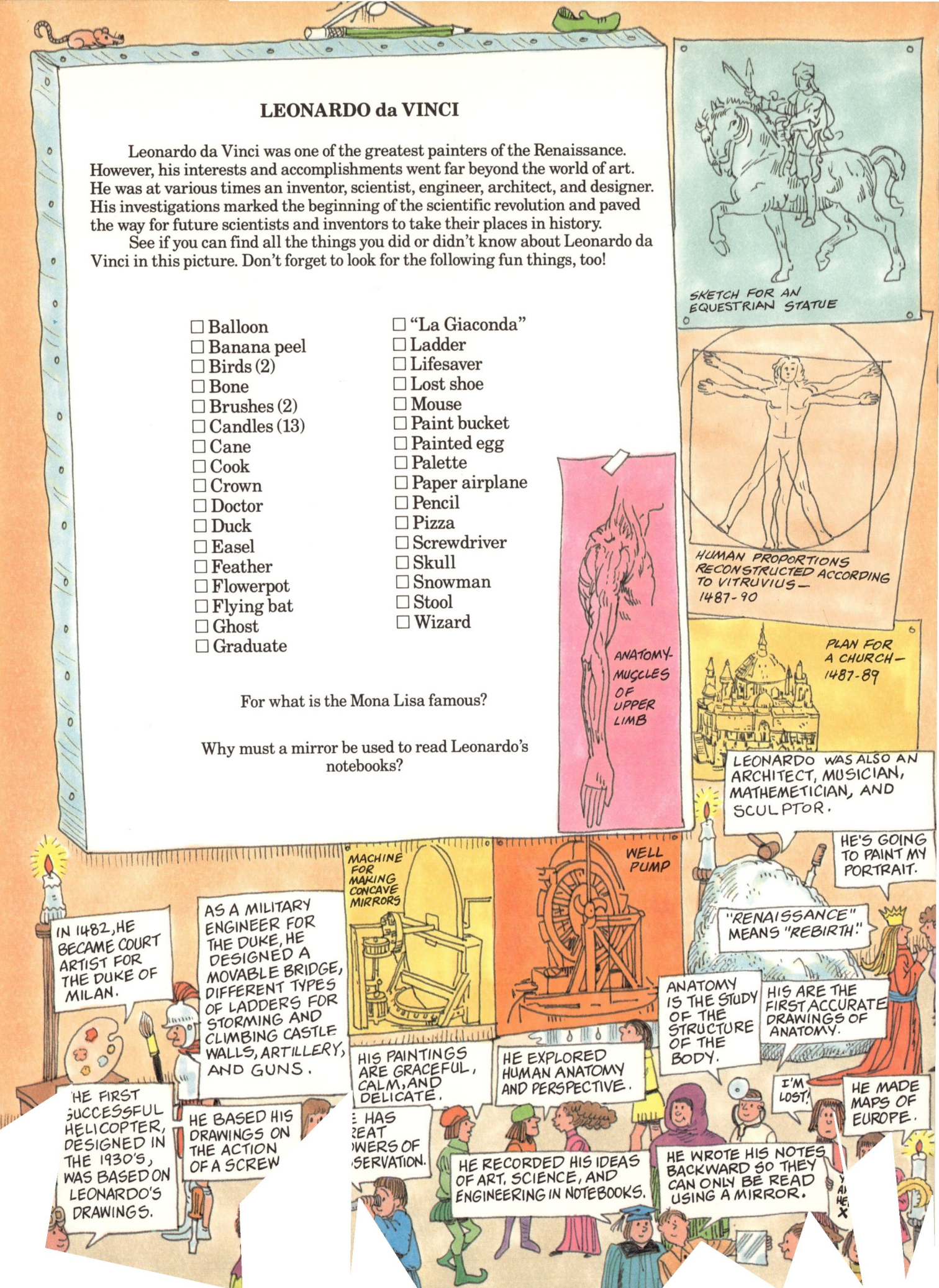

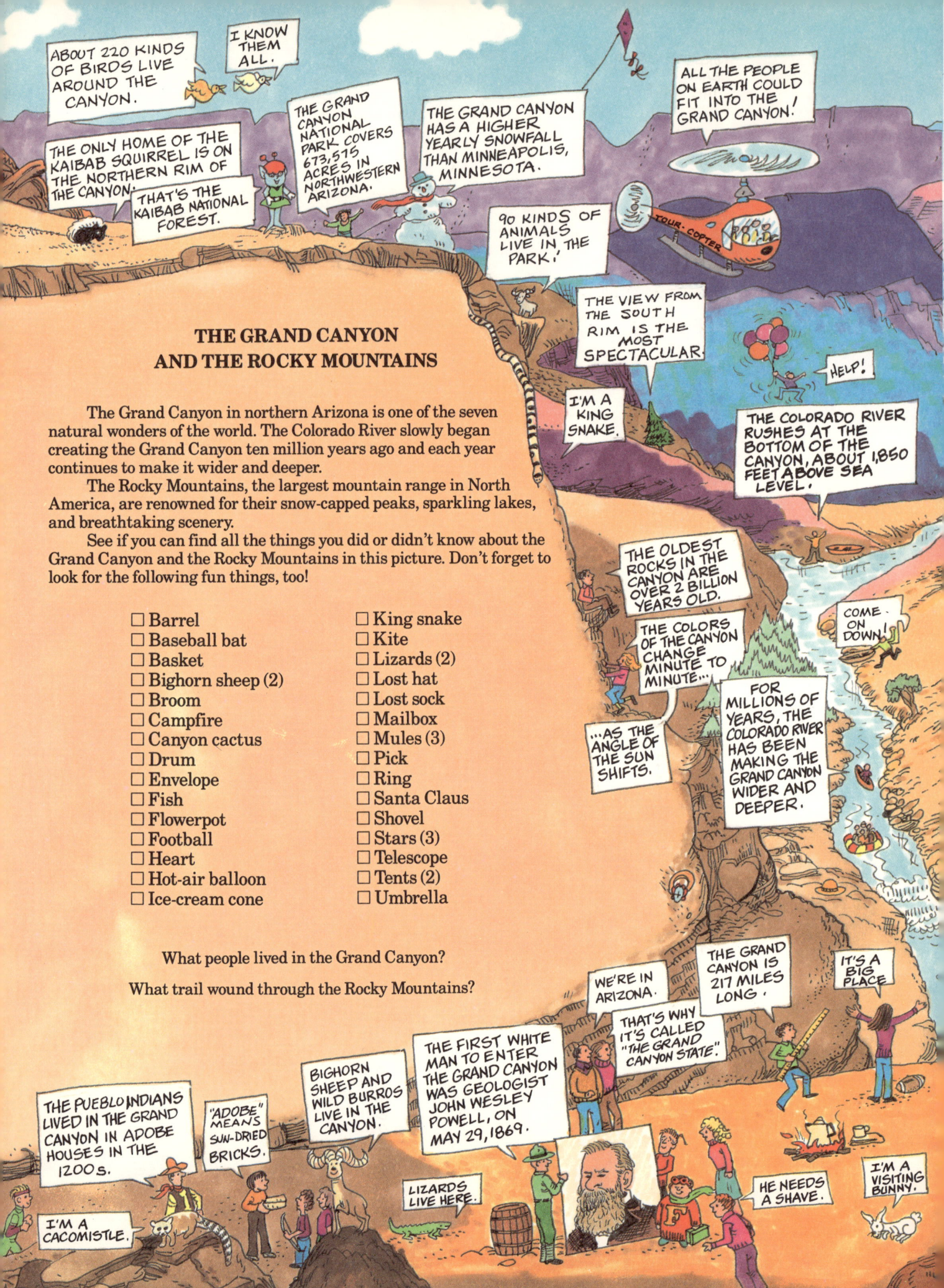

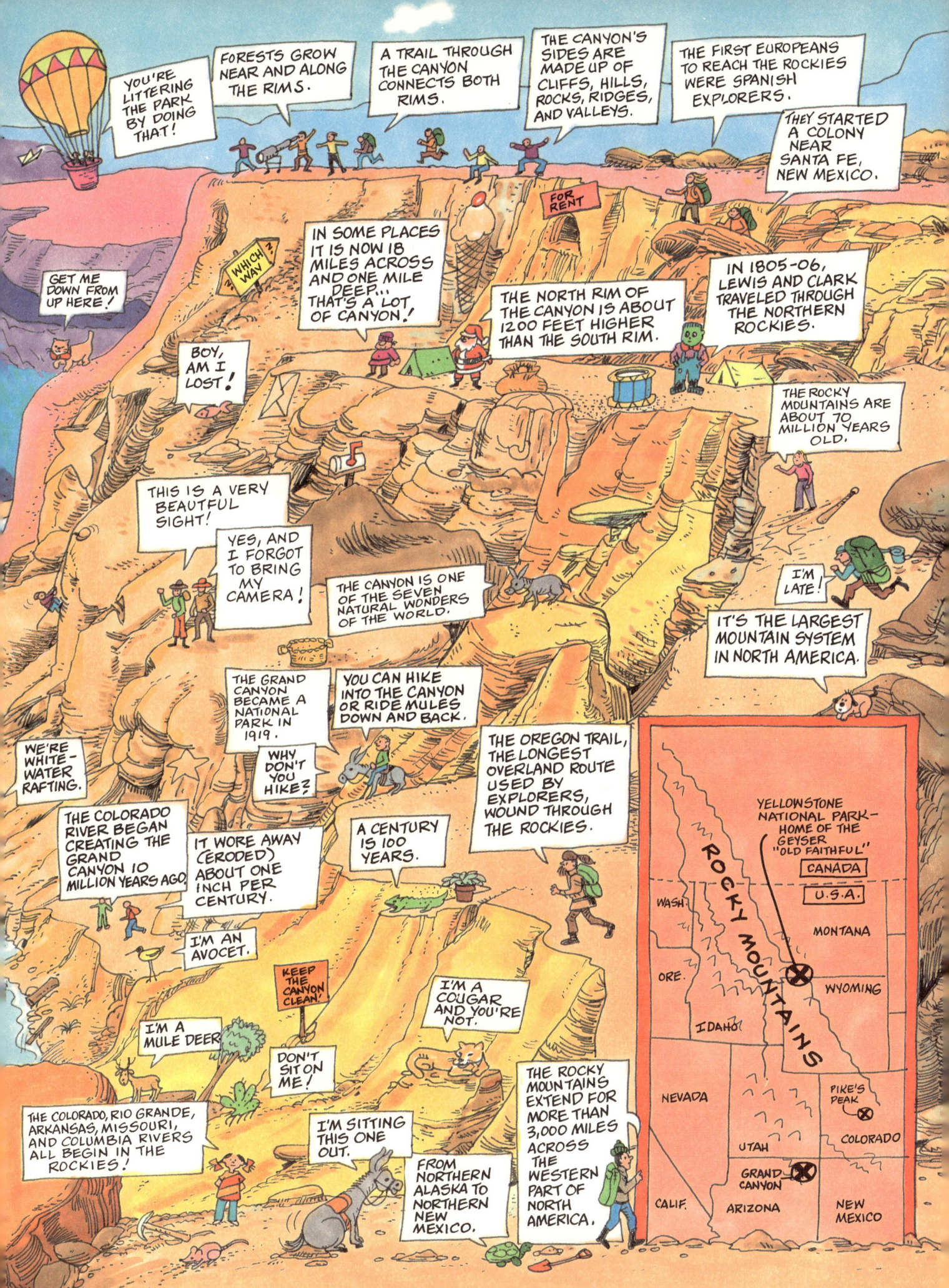

CHRISTOPHER COLUMBUS

Christopher Columbus was one of the greatest explorers of all time. In 1492, he left Spain and set sail for Asia with his three ships, the Nina, the Pinta, and the Santa Maria. Columbus never made it to the East Indies. Instead, he discovered the New World which is known today as the Americas.

See if you can find all the things you did or didn't know about Christopher Columbus. Don't forget to look for the following fun things, too!

- ☐ Arrows (2)
- ☐ Barrel
- ☐ Basket
- ☐ Bone
- ☐ Duck
- ☐ Egg
- ☐ Fish (4)
- ☐ Flower
- ☐ Hummingbird
- ☐ Jack-o'-lantern
- ☐ Key
- ☐ Laundry
- ☐ Moustache
- ☐ Octopus
- ☐ Parrot
- ☐ Periscope
- ☐ Pig
- ☐ Sea serpent
- ☐ Sick sailor
- ☐ Snake
- ☐ Spaceship
- ☐ Spears
- ☐ Sword
- ☐ T-shirt
- ☐ Telescope
- ☐ Tire
- ☐ Turtle
- ☐ Wooden leg

Who helped finance the trip?
How many voyages did Columbus make?